SOLARTOPIA!
Our Green-Powered Earth, A.D. 2030

Harvey Wasserman's Solartopia "is the good, brave renewable world of sustainability, dignity, prosperity and freedom… It is beautiful, tangible, credible, necessary, and do-able." - **Robert F. Kennedy, Jr.,** - from the *Introduction*

"The dream of a green-powered 'Solartopian' planet has been with us for fifty years. Harvey Wasserman shows us how we can get there, and what our beloved Earth might actually look like once we do. It is a dream worth working for."
- **Bonnie Raitt**

"Harvey Wasserman's Solartopia has made me what I previously thought impossible, optimistic." - **Kurt Vonnegut**

"In Harvey Wasserman's Solartopia, energy moves in harmony with the eco-sphere and all is well. Let's make it happen. We have decades of joyous work ahead."
- **Dennis Kucinich** U.S. Representative (D-Ohio)

"With so much to gain, and so much to lose, every one of us has to choose. I choose Solartopia!" - **John Hall** U.S. Representative (D-NY) *Still the One, Dance with Me.*

"Harvey Wasserman constantly provokes us and educates us, sometimes outrages us, often inspires us....He is always delightfully readable"
- **Howard Zinn**, *A People's History of the United States*

"Harvey Wasserman is truly an original"... - **Studs Terkel**

SOLARTOPIA! "is a real page-turner. Thanks for your vision, Harvey."
- **Dar Williams**, *The Beauty of the Rain; End of the Summer.*

D1533117

THIS IS DEDICATED TO THE POSSIBLE
---AND NECESSARY---
GLOBAL GREEN DREAM,
AND TO ALL WHO ARE MAKING IT HAPPEN.

THIS IS THE FIRST EDITION, RELEASED AT THE SUMMER SOLSTSTICE 2007, OF A SERIES TO BE PUBLISHED PERIODICALLY AS PART OF THE "SOLARTOPIAN CLOCK" TRACKING PROGRESS TO A TOTALLY-GREEN POWERED EARTH.

YOUR COMMENTS, VISUALIZATIONS, SONG LYRICS, AND VOTES ON THE SOLARTOPIAN CLOCK, ARE WELCOME AT WWW.SOLARTOPIA.ORG

FROM THE ENCYCLOPEDIA OF SOLARTOPIA, A.D. 2030

SOLARTOPIA: So-lar-to-pi-a. (accent on the first and third syllables): A once-futuristic vision, now the term attached to our global society of 2030, whose totally green hyper-efficient energy economy is supplied primarily by the "Solartopian Trinity" of wind, solar and bio-fuels, but which also embraces hydroelectric devices, wave and tidal harvesters, ocean thermal and geothermal sources, among others. Power is carried primarily by hydrogen, especially in the transportation system, and by electricity.

In its more general uses, the term Solartopia identifies a world now totally free of fossil and nuclear fuels, which have been permanently banned.

In historic practice, the Solartopian focus on renewable energy has expanded to embrace a model in which all forms of pollution have been eliminated, along with the production of anything that cannot be entirely recycled. Social and political reforms have followed in tandem, along with the transformation of the post-modern corporation.

First popularized early in the new millennium, the term Solartopia came to be synonymous with the larger goals of the ultimately successful global grassroots movement for a fully sustainable post-pollution economy. Its use over time has come to embrace phrases such as "the Solartopian Vision," "The Post-Fossil/Nuclear Solartopian Society," "Pollution-Free Solartopia," "Solartopian Windiana," "the Solartopian Trinity," etc.

In their early manifestations, such visions were viewed as marginal, unrealistic and even frivolous. But in the second decade of the new millennium, in the face of extreme economic and ecological peril, it became clear that without turning the Solartopian ideals into tangible realities, humankind could not survive.

And so it happened…

SOLARTOPIA!

OUR GREEN-POWERED EARTH

A.D. 2030

Science says we face global ecological catastrophe. Harvey Wasserman envisions a way out.

SOLARTOPIA! shows how we can save the planet with available technology using smart examples and simple language accessible to readers of all ages, from high schoolers to college activists and from homeowners to corporate executives.

There is no longer any scientific dissent that global warming is upon us, and that its impacts will be catastrophic. The good news is that we have the scientific and technical ability to avert its gravest outcomes. Furthermore, all the steps we need to take to avoid global warming are steps we ought to be taking anyhow, to reduce dependence on foreign oil, improve our national security, our prosperity and our health.

As early as 1952 Harry Truman's legendary Paley Commission proposed that the United States lead the world by building an economy based on renewables, and on January 16, 2000, the National Renewable Energy Laboratory issued a draft report confirming that between 99% and 124% of the electricity consumed by the United States could be supplied by renewables by the year 2020. That's a decade short of Wasserman's Solartopian ideal. In purely technical terms, there is no doubt everything "fantasized" in this book could—and should—happen. Only foot-dragging in Washington and in the corporate board rooms has denied us this future.

Even today the minions of coal, oil, nukes and gas caution that another half-century must pass before green energy can even make a dent. That would be a full century beyond the first Presidential prediction.

But the renewables industry is defying those dark predictions. The worldwide wind industry, for example, is already beyond the $10 billion per annum mark and growing at 25-35% per year worldwide. Far more new wind capacity is being built and installed worldwide than nuclear power.

Likewise the photovoltaic (PV) industry, which converts sunlight directly to electricity, is booming into a multi-billion-dollar bonanza and already exploding Wall Street expectations.

Biofuels, including corn-based ethanol and soy diesel, are transforming into major industries and already making the transition from annual food crops to "incredible inedibles" like switchgrass, poplar trees and hemp, that don't have to be sprayed, fertilized and replanted every year.

SOLARTOPIA! emphasizes wind, solar and biofuels as the exciting path to economic and ecological prosperity. Today we squander our national treasury and the lives of America's military men and women to ensure the flow of fossil fuels that are destroying our planet's air and water supply and empowering the world's worst dictators and terrorists. Non-renewable feedstocks are linear, capital-intensive and ultimately unsupportable. Their cash-flow goes just one-way: deep into the non-renewable, terrorist-funding black hole that has sucked so much out of the world economy, and especially that of the United States.

Not surprisingly Wasserman, an old-time nuclear activist who coined the term "no nukes" in the 1970s, points out that the popular panacea of nuclear power is not a realistic solution. The first atomic reactor opened at Shippingport, Pennsylvania in 1957. Despite fifty years of promises the industry and its boosters have still not solved the problems of nuclear waste, toxic emissions, catastrophic meltdowns and potential terror attacks. While renewables show fifty years of rapid advance, nuclear power backers have left a dismal track record of fifty years of failure to bring us the most catastrophically expensive form of energy ever devised.

While extractive fossil and nuclear energies decimate local and larger economies, renewables are already creating millions of jobs worldwide. They support the communities in which they're built. They offer immense paybacks in terms of saved energy costs, enhanced ecological wealth and internal recycling of community-based resources.

We are already seeing solarization projects that come in ahead of schedule, under budget, and with immense benefits—both measurable and intangible—to the communities that choose to go that route.

Only political leadership and will can save us from the certain doom of "business as usual" and take the leap of green power and sustainability and allow us to reclaim the resources now squandered on war and waste—the inevitable by-products of fossil fuels and nuclear power.

Wasserman's Solartopia is the good, brave renewable world of sustainability, dignity, prosperity and freedom. It means converting the free fuel of the sun and wind into an inexhaustible supply of wealth while creating good jobs, prosperous communities and a real chance at a just society.

This book offers a first truly accessible vision of what the outcome might look like. It is beautiful, tangible, credible, necessary, and do-able. Wasserman treats us to a hypothetical plane ride in 2030 in a craft built with hardware and blueprints which are available today. So fasten your seatbelts for this exciting ride on Wasserman's H-bio-PV H-airliner and prepare to land in Solartopia! …

-Robert F. Kennedy, Jr.

Today's Flight Plan:

From Hamburg…

…To Honolulu.

WONDERFUL

SOLARTOPIAN

COPENHAGEN!

From the heights of our hybrid "H-airliner," the view of Solartopia's very first green-powered urban Eden is magnificent and magical.

Denmark's beloved capital city, our "Friendly Old Queen of the Sea," stretches out beneath us in regal grace. Her solar-paneled rooftops gleam in the gorgeous dawn.

In a stunning emerald and gold checkerboard, they are offset by ten thousand square patches of leafy, fertile "gardens in the sky."

With their Solartopian siblings in cities everywhere---from New York to New Delhi, from Beijing to Bogota, from Tashkent to Dublin, from Capetown to Moscow--these regenerating rooftops are the upturned face of our reborn green-powered Earth, circa. 2030. They are the sustainable airborne organic gardens that help feed and recreate the body and soul of our brave renewable world.

Along the Baltic shore, turn-of-the-century turbines---our kids call them "breeze geezers"---spin in frigid northern gusts. The air is sparkling clear. The sea's a healthy, soothing blue.

Denmark has led us into Solartopia. So has Germany, from which we have just ascended. Norway and Iceland, looming in our flight path, have also played their parts.

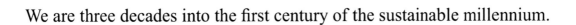

We are three decades into the first century of the sustainable millennium.

We treasure these gentle emerald economies. They brought our battered Mother Earth back from the brink of economic ruin and ecological Apocalypse, into a golden age of peerless prosperity and natural balance.

To say we fly with great reverence is to understate our gratitude.

These cold northern nations were thrice ravaged by World War and climate chaos. Having seen the face of eco-suicide, they renounced it wholeheartedly. Instead, the New Solartopians have consummated a marriage: economic prosperity fueled by Earth-friendly technologies, wed to a culture of natural efficiency and mutual respect.

In concert they launched the global solar revolution that doused the fires of climate chaos while raising the spirits of natural wealth and abundant health.

With a decisive burst of creative genius and political aplomb, the early Solartopians, to whom we owe so much, have built a marvelous post-pollution paradigm.

Getting here required a breathtaking escape from the hideous abyss of fossil/nuke addiction.

But at the brink of the Apocalypse, with Mother Nature a blink away from pulling the plug, the better angels of our souls saw the Big Light, and did what had to be done.

BYE-BYE KING C.O.N.G.

In the Age of Nukes and Oil, the natural bounty and cerebral alchemy that gave Solartopia its long-overdue birth were widely dismissed with skepticism and scorn.

Even as eco-disaster engulfed the planet, nay-sayers harped on "insurmountable" technical barriers and "impossible" political hurdles. For "King C.O.N.G."---Coal, Oil, Nukes and Gas---there were, above all, investments to protect.

What we now call King CONG was a corporate cabal of desert sheiks and petro-sharks, military madmen and jihad fanatics. With grim disdain for life itself, the monster they created coated the planet with fossil filth.

The "March of the Melt-Downs" added a catastrophic glaze of radioactive poison. Its silent death toll still kills millions.

Multiple crises in air and water, food and climate, poverty and filth, plunged us toward a ghastly end.

For some, the Exxon Valdez, Three Mile Island and Chernobyl rang the wake-up bells. For others, it was the terror attacks of September 11, 2001, followed by 2005's global-warmed Hurricane Katrina and the monumental incompetence that sank New Orleans.

Amidst the chaos, it dawned on our species that we were on the brink. And that going green might be better for business than dropping dead.

Few understood that the seismic shift to green technologies would transcend even the transformation sparked by personal computers and the worldwide web that made it possible.

The energy giants and their bloviating minions dismissed it all with searing contempt...at least in public.

In private, some weren't so sure. As the tipping point became clear, King CONG developed a lethal schizophrenia. With their immense resources, some fossil/nuke giants pioneered many of the breakthroughs that made Solartopia possible. But they also quietly grabbed up and buried key

patents, delaying their development. Some of these advances were their very own, like the infamous Electric Vehicle (EV) developed and then destroyed by General Motors.

Meanwhile they washed themselves in green, advertising an affinity for solar energy and boasting of a commitment to a clean planet.

It was a confusing charade, meant to deflect the anger of an alarmed populace while buying time to wring the last few dimes out of their obsolete inventories.

When push came to shove---no matter what they said in public---most CONG corporations fought the decentralized nature of renewable energy.

Above all, they knew that as long as there was no true accounting for the damage they did to the public health and environment, fossil and nuclear fuels would appear to be "cheaper" than renewables. Nuke power's taxpayer-financed protection from true liability for catastrophic accidents and terror attacks was the ultimate symbol of this lethal dysfunction.

But some of the wiser CONG companies---the ones that survived, at least in part---also realized that Solartopia was inevitable. As was the transformation of the corporation.

When the moment came, some were ready....or so they thought

Our Brave Renewable World

This morning our huge hybrid H-airliner sails through the pollution-free air above Scandinavia.

It's not entirely soundless. But this sun-feathered bio-bird moves like a sprite compared to the filthy kerosene-fired flying fossils that befouled the 20th Century. Those mega-polluters have all been scrapped. Every piece of them has been recycled into something better.

Like so much else in Solartopia, our ultra-light high flier was once considered an "engineering impossibility."

Today, its technical name is "H-bio-PV hybrid."

The "bio" refers to the core power provided by farm-grown fuels. The fermentation of Earth's fastest-growing, most cellulose-intense crops gives us a great green liquor that far exceeds the energy content of any fossil fuel to which we were once so catastrophically addicted.

The "H" is for renewably-produced hydrogen. When mixed with our base bio-fuels, these potent proton-electron pairs provide the extra zip that flies us at speeds once thought impossible for ships this big.

The "PV" is for the solar cells that line our wings and fuselage. These high-tech photovoltaic collectors are everywhere in Solartopia. They cleanly and quietly convert sunlight to electricity, which in this case gives our flying chariot a vital backup.

But "H-bio-PV hybrid" never really sang to younger Solartopians. Thus the jokey, affectionate "H-airliner" nickname.

Early green advocates realized that beating King CONG would demand more than just rational argument and great organizing. It would need intellectual risk-taking, and that irreverent yippie magic that transcends obsolete paradigms in a single bound. "Any revolution without humor is a turn in the wrong direction" sang a movement that faced humankind's darkest times with inexplicable but immutable (and essential) optimism.

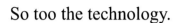

So too the technology.

Like all else in our brave renewable world, the hyper-efficient jet fuel mix of organic plant residue with renewable hydrogen and solar cells was long ago dismissed as "voodoo physics" by lavishly funded "experts" who always knew more than anyone else. Many of these professional nay-sayers surfaced as TV commentators. Their endlessly erroneous arrogance is still the stuff of Solartopian satire.

All the technology that was ever needed for a post-pollution world was available in 2007, when the term *Solartopia* took off. All the advances that now seem so spectacular flowed easily and organically from what was readily available at the turn of the new century. And the "impossible" vision of "those solar fools" is now the ultimate Solartopian cash cow.

It took no magic wand to get us to where we are now...only what Albert Einstein might have called "a holistic new way of thinking."

Utopian seers inspired grassroots pioneers who paved the way for solar scientists and green engineers, followed, inevitably, by prescient financiers.

And, of course, Solartopia's first worst enemies now claim credit for making it all happen.

From Proton Palace to Pure Efficiency

Our slender solar wing sails sweetly over green/gold Copenhagen. Both gleam in the gorgeous morning sun.

Like our H-airliner, Denmark is supremely efficient. She is prosperous and clean, safe and fair.

In the bad Oil Days, we humans beat our Mother Earth almost to oblivion. Climate chaos, runaway radiation and a poisoned biosphere delivered what seemed to be terminal blows to our maternal home. Huge dead zones festered like tumors at land and sea. Countless species (including our own) teetered at the brink. Too many tumbled over.

Even now, our beloved planet gently reels… and slowly heals.

As she does, we prosper.

At dawn we soared out of Hamburg, the post-petroleum heart of the German "Green Giant," the first Solartopian super-power.

Hamburg claims Earth's first H-station. Way back on January 13, 1999, Mayor Ortwin Runde could barely contain himself. "The streets will be quiet," he sang as he cut the ceremonial ribbon. Hamburg "will be clean, since emissions will be practically zero."

He was right. But Solartopia is hardly just about hydrogen.

Hamburg's pioneer H-fuel center proved merely the first of countless thousands. These profoundly popular "Proton Palaces" now help anchor our post-pollution planet. (As we shall see, the tourist bureau in Thousand Palms says California's H-pumps were first, and should be honored above Hamburg's. We have no horse in this petty dispute).

As widely predicted, hydrogen has become an iconic energy carrier. In millions of super-advanced Solartopian fuel cells, H delivers heat and electricity, multi-purpose power and the much-needed by-product of pure fresh water.

As with the jet in which we now so cleanly fly, hydrogen also helps move much of the world's transport.

But H does not dance alone.

In the first years of the new millennium, hydrogen was hyped as a miracle fuel. It inspired utopian screeds heralding a new era of H-energy. Incredibly, there was even talk of building nuclear power plants to create hydrogen for automobiles. Some Solartopians still chuckle about that one, though it's painful, like laughing with a broken rib.

For much of the hype about H was an illusion. Hydrogen is a medium of energy transfer, not a fuel. It burns cleanly and efficiently. In fuel cells, it delivers power as if by magic. But first, H must be rendered into usable form. And that costs money. And resources.

Producing hydrogen with nuke reactors would have further threatened our prospects for survival.

Most Solartopians can no longer bear to describe the horrific demise of atomic energy. The March of the Melt-Downs was an unGodly string of ghastly disasters. Building and running nuclear generators was just a short-cut to handing terrorists---and incompetent utilities---their very own nukes of mass destruction.

Terror and error became the twin towers of reactor disaster.

Global warming was the end-game. New Orleans was sunk into the sea by climate chaos and astounding incompetence. The ice caps melted. Runaway climate cycles, like the Pacific's El Nino, became mass killers.

Poisoned and plundered, the oceans metastasized into gargantuan stretches of marine dead zones, where fish and sea grasses sighed and died. Water, food, climate and air soared to the top of the Solartopian imperative.

With the Danes and Germans in the lead, an irradiated, exhausted and angry world finally grabbed the reins… and the rains.

Proton production went green. Renewable H joined wind power, solar-generated electricity and eco-friendly bio-fuels in the "Green Trinity" that, with spotless efficiency, converts nature's bounty into usable fuel and economic plenty.

Balanced atop this sun-powered troika, the new millennium found its center in a stable, reliable, renewable, ultra-efficient energy base.

As with so many historic waves of technological advance, this one was both astonishing and predictable. In the late 20th Century, the personal computer and worldwide web set the stage for a post-industrial transformation. Computing power was based on the same silicon as solar cells, and shared some of the same path-breaking pioneers, such as William Heronemus, Buckminster Fuller, Stanford and Iris Ovshinsky.

With the new millennium, global-networked computing capability escaped the binary limits of its initial incarnation. Its powers multiplied again and again, and then again and yet again.

The eco-sciences advanced in tandem.

Those who thought they could predict the "hard limits" of the soft path wound up bewildered... and bedazzled. Those smart enough to bet ahead of the green power curve were generously enriched...and eternally grateful.

The Solartopian Trinity

"Anything that burns can be replaced with hydrogen." This ancient prophecy from Stan Ovshinsky now defines all our public transport.

Our ships at sea, the buses, trolleys, trains, and even the few remaining private automobiles...they all move with hydrogen. In part.

From Hamburg to Thousand Palms and beyond, a new global H-distribution net has evolved in synch with a radically revamped electric grid. Production is epic.

But hydrogen alone does not power the hyper-complex post-pollution infrastructure on which our global billions rely.

Instead, it flows in tandem with the Solartopian Trinity: wind, solar and bio-fuels.

Like any three-legged structure, each has its role to play.

Take bio-fuels.

Ethanol, bio-diesel and their farm-raised siblings animate much of our Solartopian economy. They are critical pieces of Solartopia's power pie. But they are no more a magic bullet than hydrogen.

In their early incarnations, ethanol was based on corn, and bio-diesel on soy. They have been important bridging fuels.

But too many forests were cleared to grow them. Too much fertilizer was poured on already over-farmed fields, which were then over-worked with too many tractors aimed at too much short-term gain.

There was a brief stab at genetically engineering crops for energy, which failed catastrophically.

But the real barriers came with using annual food crops for energy. Humankind is still threatened by hunger. Corn and soy are now firmly retrenched where they belong---at the dinner table.

Today, the "incredible in-edibles" rule the energy roost. Switchgrass, hemp, poplars and some surprise breeds, like miscanthus, kudzu and algae, are among Solartopia's favorite bio-fuel perennials. They grow without chemical pesticides, herbicides or petro-fertilizers. They flourish on marginal, reclaimed land. They demand little mechanical cultivation or energy inputs (except sunlight). Their true net gain is epic.

And so they provide a core fuel for our trains and trolleys, cars and bio-planes.

But they don't work alone.

The H-airliner in which we now fly relies on ultra-light, ultra-strong solarized materials. Virtually all Solartopian vehicles are coated with photovoltaic (PV) veneer. Such shells began as rigid silicon-based cells that convert sunlight to electricity. There are still billions of crystalline PV cells in use.

But as Solartopia took off, ultra-advanced "amorphous" PV found its way into window glass and roofing shingles, house paint and finishing materials. Ovshinsky's pioneer Ovonics factories near Detroit still churn out billions of floppy shingles that top off a whole new generation of green buildings.

Today there is hardly a single exposed surface on any Solartopian structure or vehicle that does not somehow generate electricity. A critical stream of electrons trickles out from every home and office. Many a hybrid H-airliner has been saved by the electric rivulets flowing from the PV on its wings and fuselage. (They also warm our breakfast, our morning coffee, and the seats on which we sit).

Nor do Solartopian people movers stall out on the highway. Today, all vehicles, by law, carry enough reserve PV-generated electricity to go that last mile to help. No bus or train, trolley or car is ever so far from an emergency way-station that it can't be reached with solar juice generated on-board.

Nor do countless victims die each year in gas-fired car crashes.

Waste Not, Want Not

For a new generation of Solartopian geeks, the latest renewable fuels seem downright sexy. But it was hyper-efficiency that laid our sustainable green foundation.

In the Twilight of Nukes and Oil, the west wasted fully half the juice it produced. In their primitive, pre-Solartopian incarnations, China and India--- today's monster green economies---were worst of all.

Back then, the gap between what Solartopians dreamed of producing and what the world actually consumed made it all seem impossible.

But people began keeling over dead from China's brown, filthy air. The wrath of climate chaos drowned millions and starved more. The Solartopian Trinity became less an impossible dream than a fervent prayer for deliverance.

And it demanded, first and foremost, that we "face the waste."

To avoid extinction, ultra-efficiency became a vital necessity.

And so there came super-stingy Light Emitting Diode (L.E.D.) lighting that runs on a tiny fraction of what Edison's first bulbs required. Super-compact fluorescents, ultra-light composites, mega-efficient manufacturing, totally tight solar building designs---they all help Solartopia squeeze every available electron out of a dying fossil/nuke paradigm.

Super-conducting, mag-lev and other "breakthrough" nega-watt technologies have turned the post-pollution universe into the ultimate energy miser.

The iconic allegory is the desperate 1969 return of the crippled Apollo 13 spacecraft. This primitive manned probe was on its way to the moon (now a popular spa) when disaster struck. All but killed by an explosion, the three Apollo astronauts could only limp back to Earth by preserving every electron their damaged craft could muster.

Scientists and engineers at home base tortured one scale model after another, desperately seeking ways to save. The imperiled aviators knew every miniscule resource left on board was infinitely precious.

By eliminating every hint of waste, the Apollo 13 astronauts made it home. So far, so have we.

Today we revere Apollo 13 as a herald to all we've endured since the climate crisis went critical. Its images are everywhere in Solartopia. The Ron Howard/Tom Hanks 1995 film classic has been mandatory viewing for all high school students since 2010.

All Solartopian machines are "Apollo-efficient." Nothing---NOTHING!---on "Spaceship Earth" is manufactured that cannot be totally and entirely recycled or composted.

Under extreme penalties mandated by the "Apollo 13 Laws," no factory, no consumer item, no vehicle, no article of clothing is produced with even one component that will not mutate into something re-usable once its first incarnation is done. (The Apollo Alliance, an early green labor group, trains a unionized workforce to guarantee enforcement).

The trash that once defiled our streets and highways is now deemed far too valuable to leave lying around. The waste that poisoned our global economy is unimaginable. The lethal addiction to hyper-consumption that threatened to end our stay on Earth is yesterday's absurdity.

So is an architectural profession that simply could not grasp the most basic essentials of solar design. Suddenly, they got a social and economic ultimatum: go green, or get lost.

Builders who could not seem to spell "efficiency" or "south-facing" or "solarization" finally learned how. An entrepreneurial army of genius green zealots now builds us dazzling new spaces that produce energy rather than consuming it.

Code enforcers passionately police even ancient structures for leaking heat and errant joules. The ancient indifference to waste has gone the way of exploding lunar probes and imperiled astronauts.

Against all odds…Spaceship Earth has safely landed! It's tight as a drum. It pays its own way.

Don't Paint Your Blimp with Jet Fuel

So for decades now, for pennies on the dollar, humankind has thrived on the ultra-lean "Apollo 13 Energy Diet."

This revolution in hyper-efficiency set the stage for the alchemical mix of wind, solar, bio-fuel and their sibling natural sources that power our world.

An early surprise was the use of H in passenger planes like this one. When debate about a hydrogen economy first opened in earnest, most eyes turned to the automobile. The "Hypercar" would transcend filthy fossil-fired internal combustion private vehicles with clean/green H-powered people movers.

Auto-makers pursued the H dream with varying degrees of commitment. Fuel cells were all the early rage. But Germany's BMW took a daring position for internal combustion engines that seamlessly switched from gasoline to hydrogen. When metal hydride H-storage and a new generation of batteries came of age, the gamble proved truly prophetic.

Solartopia's ultra-efficient downtown/suburban transit systems (first they were "trolleys," then "light rail," now we call them trolleys again) speed along on clean green fuels. So do the lush, super-sleek passenger trains that once again connect our cities.

Today we wince in disbelief over the absurdity of using fossil-burning automobiles to move people from one urban area to another. Or (even sillier) to get around within the cities and suburbs themselves. Many young Solartopians still don't believe it was ever done.

The "sleeper" was the passenger plane. Since 1937 the dominant image of H-powered air travel was the infamous dirigible Hindenburg. Its spectacular New Jersey fire killed 36 people. Ever since the unforgettable radio-broadcast frenzy that accompanied it down, H-powered flight has evoked images of death and doom.

But the Hindenburg fire was not caused by hydrogen. An American researcher named Addison Bain proved long ago that the dirigible's skin was coated with highly flammable chemicals. A simple spark, likely from lightning, flared it to ruin.

Some of the H inside the balloon did burn, said Bain. Most just floated away.

Many passengers died. But many who might have been obliterated by an actual explosion did not.

Bain's moral of the story: "Don't paint your airship with jet fuel."

Once fully understood, the Hindenburg actually showed that air travel powered by H-bio hybrid fuel is far safer than it was in those primitive clunkers fired by kerosene.

The harshest example was at Tenerife in 1987. When two jets collided, more than 500 people perished in a hellish petro-pyre. If those jets had been

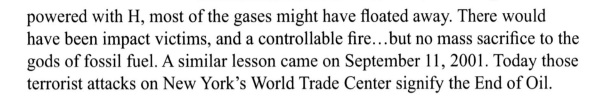

powered with H, most of the gases might have floated away. There would have been impact victims, and a controllable fire...but no mass sacrifice to the gods of fossil fuel. A similar lesson came on September 11, 2001. Today those terrorist attacks on New York's World Trade Center signify the End of Oil.

For all the wrong reasons, politicians and the petro-barons fought the obvious. Debate still rages over exactly what brought those towers down, and who was responsible.

But one thing we know: the physical impact of the hijacked jets slamming into the twin towers did not cause them to collapse.

Some official reports still blame prolonged super-hot jet fuel fires that weakened the towers' structural steel. A wide range of unofficial theories---none charitable to those in power at the time---offer other explanations.

But if those terrorists had tried what they did with one of today's ultra-light, hybrid-fueled H-airliners, 9/11/01 would have been a very different story.

September 11 was a horrific price to pay for addiction to mid-east oil. With the Solartopian Revolution in efficiency and renewables, global terrorism has been de-fanged and de-funded. The politicians who allowed it to happen by failing to get us off oil have been discredited, denounced, discarded.

The futile, catastrophic petro-wars that followed in Iraq, Iran and Afghanistan, Mexico and Venezuela, Russia and Canada, made the inevitable flight to Solartopia that much more urgent, especially as America plunged to petro-bankruptcy.

The reading racks on our H-airliner hold no magazines featuring the sad young faces of soldiers dying for oil. Breathless features on Arab sheiks and super-rich petro-sharks are long gone.

Today's heroes and heroines are the activists and organizers, engineers and architects, biologists and eco-entrepreneurs navigating us through King CONG's hellish wake. Thanks to them, we fly clean and quiet, safe and cheap. Petro-terrorism is yesterday's nightmare.

Flying the Eco-Friendly Skies

Though few noticed at the time, 9/11/2001 accidentally opened a vital viewpoint on the ecological impacts of fossil-fired air travel.

For three days after the attack, US commercial air traffic simply stopped.

The upper atmosphere was suddenly relieved of the industry's relentless emissions. Through that uniquely clean three-day window, science saw with shocking clarity the devastating impact of fossil fuel residues directly injected into the upper atmosphere.

Sooner or later, the experts warned, it had to stop. The biosphere could take only so much. We had reached the limit.

A new mix of biofuels for base-load power, super-charged with renwably-produced Hydrogen, boosted by PV-generated electricity, evolved as an early answer for sustainable air travel.

Even more sophisticated mixes, with ingredients as yet undiscovered, may soon leap ahead. But for now, the upper atmosphere heals, the ozone layer regenerates, we seem to have a future.

Silent Heights

If even better fuels should come, they must be more than just clean. They must sustain or improve the near-soundlessness Solartopian H-airliners have achieved.

At first, the stunning quietude of H-bio-PV hybrid air travel was greeted as a miracle. For those living in flight paths, working in airports, or flying frequently, a quiet new world had dawned.

They danced in the runways!…   They threw away their earplugs!!…   They could hear… REALLY HEAR… for the first time in decades!!!

The subliminal impact of all that noise was never fully understood…until it disappeared. Today, the joy of living on a planet freed from traffic hum and industrial ear pollution feeds our collective soul in ways we cannot begin to calculate.

Our kids and theirs take all that quiet for granted.

Some of us do remember how annoyingly noisy those old oil birds really were. When a promoter cranks up an antique airshow, we chuckle as our offspring hold their ears in disbelief.

But in this eco-evolved era of pristine skies and precious silence, such indulgences are rare.

Those old air clunkers mix well only with the few remaining internal combustion automobiles and other offal from the bad oil days. In the funerary piles of recyclable scrap, an awful imposition disappeared forever.

Blimp-flown Wind Warriors

Our flight path from Hamburg has carried us across the Baltic. The cold, clear northern sea bristles with gigantic platforms that frame huge ultra-modern Danish turbines. These are the whirly work horses of Europe's pioneer green prosperity.

Many were installed with Solartopian blimps. The realization that H was not the Hindenburg's murderer begot a brand new breed of gigantic zeppelins.

The romance of long-distance travel on these gentle giants has been irresistible. A whole new niche in luxury tourism has grown around globe-trotting sky-whales.

They are far slower than the jet in which we fly today. But they're as gently relaxing as they are slow and scenic. Newly-weds love them. It's hard to beat a glass-bottomed glide through the very friendly skies for a memorable H-oneymoon.

The real money in Solartopian blimps comes from ferrying big, heavy machinery and building components. Many a Solartopian skyscraper has been topped off with a fancy roof cap dangled down from a big balloon.

Likewise the giant nacelle. These are the turbine housings for the gigantic wind arrays that perch in deep water or stand alone in remote mountain regions.

For years a serious barrier to increasing turbine size was the challenge of topping off ever-taller towers and ocean platforms. There's only so high a crane can reach, only so wide and heavy a load a country road can accommodate.

The air knows no such limits. Nor do blimps.

The skeptics scoffed. But most of today's new wind turbines are erected---and serviced---from computer-stabilized H-airships that hover and deliver. From the Hindenburg's ashes---now that we understand them---a great good has arisen.

The Breeze Geezers

Fading behind us, Queen Copenhagen basks in her gold-green glory.

Throughout Europe, ancient infrastructures like hers have been saved from acid decimation. The toxic emissions that hideously scarred them, and even threatened to bring them down, are no more. They've been washed clean of the noxious rains and radioactive poisons spewed from Chernobyl and the ensuing nuke disasters that came oh-so-close to ending human life altogether.

Instead, these graceful urban habitats nestle safely downwind from thousands of commercial wind turbines strung along the coast and scattered in the Baltic like Loch Ness silhouettes adorned with twirly beanies. From up here they seem like child's pinwheels, playfully perched around miniature cities.

These sleek, slender towers and turbines happen to be hugely profitable. They are the financial backbone of Europe's renewable retrenchment, the economic miracle that's delivered such gratifying prosperity to all Solartopians wise enough to invest early and often.

Denmark reveres its sea-side hedge of once-young wind machines...the ones the kids now scorn (like their hopelessly obsolete parents) as "breeze geezers." Built at the turn of the century, by 2030 standards they are downright quaint. Far bigger ones dwarf them at every turn.

But these creaky oldsters can still move electrons. In tandem with their bigger, younger progeny, they produce the electricity, the hydrogen and the fresh water that make human life possible.

Denmark's first coastal turbines were installed within a few years on either side of what was once called "Y2K." These elderly miniatures are a piddling 200 or 300 feet high. The blades are shorter still. Their capacity is two megawatts each, or even less. Some provide enough juice for just a few hundred homes. They are museum pieces.

But if their scale is tiny, their durability is legend.

They were scheduled to die in thirty years. But many will spin out cheap electricity for a half-century or more, especially with the new organic lubricants now greasing their innards. Signs of fatigue are few, except among those hopeful investors itching to grab their sites for bigger machines.

But ownership of Denmark's wind industry is arranged through an intricate mosaic of independent citizens and collective communities. All get a steady source of income with which they can buy their cheap green power…and a few groceries to boot.

This grassroots ownership scheme helped the Danes dodge the multi-national monopolies that so hideously plagued the 20th Century. Free of the fossil/nuke corporate domination that drove America to ruin---and that threatened to take down the rest of the planet---it was a Danish turbine blade that first pierced mighty King CONG's rotting armor.

Loving Our Baseload "Green Sea Monsters"

Out in the Baltic, the North Sea and the North Atlantic, the "green sea monsters" reign supreme. Their giant frames tower hundreds of feet above the frigid waves. Their blades are as big as football fields.

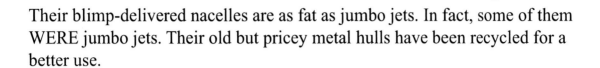

Their blimp-delivered nacelles are as fat as jumbo jets. In fact, some of them WERE jumbo jets. Their old but pricey metal hulls have been recycled for a better use.

These mega-wind warriors do the heavy lifting for northern Europe's baseload power needs. An elaborate network of submerged tubes and cables pump into the mainland an endless supply of hydrogen and electricity.

With their fossil and nuke plants long shut, the Baltic and Scandinavian states all supplement their wind with power from solar collectors, energy crops and tidal generators.

The on-shore burning of sea-made hydrogen yields vital fresh water for a global ecology still reeling from the fossil/nuke catastrophe.

To its everlasting benefit, Denmark shunned nuclear power altogether. It never squandered its wealth or health on a single commercial reactor. A grateful nation still reveres---with public statues and middle school textbooks---those 1970s "No Nukes" activists and visionaries who made that green decision happen.

With virtually no native coal or oil, the Danes aimed straight at the sun. They dodged the gargantuan capital debt that ensnared the sadly over-nuked French. With wind-power, the saying goes, Denmark "not only did good, it did very well."

King CONG scoffed. In oil-addicted alliance with middle Eastern sheiks, it feared green power's threat to its obscene petro-fortunes. War after ugly war came in the name of messianic religion and *faux* democracy.

But the driving force was oil. And the crash and burn was horrific.

A Wind Danish with Solar Strudel

The Danes' love affair with wind energy dates back centuries. Their lack of fossil deposits and "atomic allergy" became a double blessing of clean air and big money.

In the 1990s Denmark boasted four of the world's richest turbine makers. By 2005, some 10,000 Danes were shaping blades, erecting towers, welding nacelles. Even today, windmills and their trimmings comprise Denmark's biggest export.

Across the Baltic, the Germans saw the Solartopian future as clearly as they saw those Euros pouring into Danish coffers.

German economic planners knew all too well the true cost of the fossil/nuke addiction. They understood the curse of global warming. They suffered in unquiet anger from Chernobyl's lethal cloud.

Prompted by the power of its Green Party, Germany abandoned its seventeen reactors, and sought alternatives. To be sure, there were periodic corporate attempts to revive the atomic corpse.

But cooler *kopfs* always prevailed. And the decision to go green transcended just energy.

Like the Danes, Germany realized that saving the global ecology was not merely a matter of survival. It could guarantee prosperity.

So they re-engineered their economy around mandatory recycling and a manic avoidance of inefficiency in all its costly incarnations.

The Germans reasoned that pollution was just another form of waste. So they attacked it as ruthlessly as they cut costs, making huge profits---and a pivotal contribution to global sustainability.

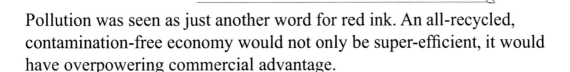

Pollution was seen as just another word for red ink. An all-recycled, contamination-free economy would not only be super-efficient, it would have overpowering commercial advantage.

Led by Denmark and Germany, the European Union became Earth's primary post-pollution provider. There were bumps and false starts. But the EU soared into a golden age of sustainable prosperity. It easily leap-frogged the "Double W Depression" that drove the U.S. to its oil-soaked, war-torn knees.

The Red, White & Blue...and Green

The green energy at the core of Europe's success mocked America's catastrophic decline.

As early as 1998, Germany blew past the US to become the number one generator of wind-driven electricity. With Danish designs and their own gear-less Enercon turbines, the Germans saturated their countryside with ever-larger, super-efficient "combines in the sky." Spain soon followed, passing the US in wind-power production just after the dawn of the millennium.

The best German wind sites were soon filled, and its industry took a temporary hit. So did Denmark's, when right-wingers briefly took power.

There were other problems. Some of northern Europe's big off-shore arrays were eaten alive by salt-water corrosion, especially in their gear boxes. Costly retrofitting gave the industry a black eye, infected by red ink.

Then came the public opposition. It took some serious contortions to argue that wind farming could harm the economy or ecology. But there will always be those who prefer to look at a pristine seascape, rather than one punctuated with towers and turbines.

And in Solartopia, scenic virginity is as much a public virtue as economic growth, even when it's green and clean.

Where the twain meets is where the wind farms do---and don't---get planted. Many have been built, and many have been stopped. The arguments rage as you read this. It is a constant tilt not likely to end in our lifetimes.

What we have learned, looking backward from 2030, is that the most important factor determining which wind farm will get built can be who owns it.

In the early days, it was fairly simple: those projects proposed by private developers and rich corporations were far more likely to arouse public ire than those owned by the public itself. That's been especially true when it comes to privately owned projects proposed for publicly-owned sites.

Solartopians have looked far more ire-free at wind machines they own as a community than at those that pour the proceeds into corporate pockets.

It's been a long time since a privately owned project---however ecologically sound--- has jumped through the needle's eye onto public land. Nobody's holding their breath until it happens again.

But we all breathe deep, thankful breaths for the tens of thousands of turbines owned by farmers and small landowners, community coops and municipal electric companies…and for the transformation they ultimately forced on King CONG.

The Wind We Drink

The huge, expansive floating platforms that spin at sea are topped by tubular frames hundreds of feet high, each housing four, six or eight massive propeller arrays. These big blades spin internal generators that produce

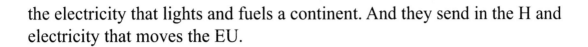

the electricity that lights and fuels a continent. And they send in the H and electricity that moves the EU.

Like most of today's European cities, Copenhagen's mass transit system moves in part with the electrons and protons piped in from endless rows of turbines that spin in the ocean breeze.

Gleaming in the sun's golden rays, thousands of rooftop panels generate still more electricity and hot water. Interspersed with those cleansing airborne gardens, they help make it healthier to breathe in Copenhagen than it has been since the Vikings began burning wood.

That also goes for the water we drink.

With gear-box corrosion problems largely solved, wind farms dot the Earth's oceans. Along with vast quantities of cheap electricity, hydrogen is also created. When it's burned, it creates the pure water that's just one of the unexpected benefits of the Solartopian Revolution. These ocean-based mega-turbines are, in their own various ways, gigantic fresh water stills.

Ironically, it was 1950s nuke submarines that first zapped sea water with electricity to make fresh water for use on board.

Using wind-driven electrolysis to turn corrosive seawater into usable quantities of fresh water seemed a complete flight of fancy...a "pipe dream" as the pundits called it.

But the potential rewards for figuring something out were immense---financially, ecologically, and in terms of basic human survival.

After all King CONG did to the world's water, it's a wonder we survived at all. The global-warmed destruction of the earth's rivers, lakes and reservoirs made water our most precious commodity.

Amidst horrific shortages, even the relatively small quantities of fresh water generated through Solartopian means became precious and pivotal.

As the new Europe boomed, producing green power became inseparable from producing "green water." As we shall see, when it came time to take down the dams and save our natural watersheds, that made all the difference.

"Too Cheap to Meter"

Banking gently northwest, we pass over the breathtaking gorges and frigid fjords of northern Scandinavia.

Norway's early glide to Solartopian prosperity came astride the powerful currents of these steep, raging streams. Its abundant hydroelectric power produced so much easy electricity, smug Norse optimists said it would someday be "too cheap to meter." So far, they are almost right.

For decades those dams made pure hydrogen for a booming fertilizer industry. So when H became a premier carrier of green energy, Norway was poised to soar past all of Europe. In the race to be totally fossil-free, Oslo sped ahead.

Norway became another kind of green pioneer with the Solartopia's first undersea "tide turbine." The 200 ton pinwheel at Kvalsund, near the Arctic circle, is basically a windmill underwater. Its three massive blades spin hard to the power of the moon and currents.

Air is light. It moves in fits and starts.

But the currents are dense and heavy… and they never stop. Nor do the tides, which reverse direction every twelve hours and 25 minutes.

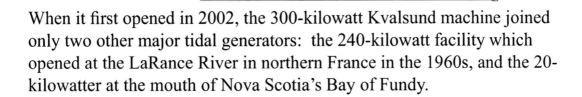

When it first opened in 2002, the 300-kilowatt Kvalsund machine joined only two other major tidal generators: the 240-kilowatt facility which opened at the LaRance River in northern France in the 1960s, and the 20-kilowatter at the mouth of Nova Scotia's Bay of Fundy.

Sturdy and simple, all three still work well.

Ecologically, they remain suspect. Like dams----so many of which we have torn down--- these tide catchers can disrupt the natural flow on which some species depend. Their ultimate impacts are still not entirely clear.

So we site them with extreme care. We watch them like hawks.

Like all other Solartopian innovations, the jury is always out on the inevitable surprise, the unintended eco-consequence.

If you want to know what we really think about the environmental costs of these tide-mills and underwater turbines, ask again in ten years. If all is going well, we'll tell you to ask again in ten more years.

Those Fascinating "Water Worms"

Whatever the ultimate eco-impact, the development of underwater tide- and current-powered generators has given green power a giant, watery leap.

Inevitable (or were they?) advances in tidal and ocean current power came with new breakthroughs in capturing energy from waves. Powered by the ceaseless up-down movement of the oceans, early wave energy devices have only two moving parts. They work as the bobbing water squishes through their pipes to turn turbines and create electricity.

These giant "water worms" are now deployed off-shore all over the planet. In some places they double as breakwaters. They vary hugely in length, girth and generating capacity. But they are simple and strong and highly productive.

Their hybrid cousins have made their way into our rivers. As the dams have come down, free-floating versions of the ocean water worms combine current, tide and wave power technologies. First developed in the early 2000s, they bob, twirl, spin… and generate power without impeding the free flow of our waterways. Over time they have replaced much of the capacity lost when Solartopia finally brought down those ancient, obsolete dams that clotted up our watery arteries.

After we figure out where to put them, the only real controversy surrounding these aquatic generators comes from those who persist in wanting to decorate them. Mostly these devices leave the factory a dull, practical gray or green or blue, meant to blend in with the waters that surround them.

But wherever they go, younger Solartopians love to paint them up in color schemes that range from merely wild to wildly obscene. As with the wind towers in the midwest, the issue of advertising has also arisen.

Needless to say, there've been a lot of angry words, and even a few arrests.

These petty artistic squabbles keep us gratefully distracted. We are a wealthy, just society, improbably calm. Every year we spend billions in our university and governmental Departments of Peace, seeking ways to stay that way.

For many of our younger people, that all translates to "smugly boring." Our kids know little of the battles fought to get here, and could often care less.

But history warns that when a generation gets antsy, no matter how good they might have it, bad things can happen. So our wisest elders have all come to the same conclusion: better to fight "graffiti wars" over the

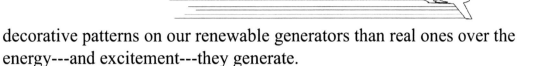

decorative patterns on our renewable generators than real ones over the energy---and excitement---they generate.

As we now say whenever we inaugurate a new array of green power stations: "Let the color wars begin!"

Ocean Co-Gen

Nor are the wave generators, whatever their hue, the only clean sources of energy to rise out of the sea.

At the Solartopian dawn, the biggest barrier to offshore wind was raising the capital to erect the arrays, especially in the Great Lakes and deep oceans. Building and anchoring huge platforms offshore, and webbing together the pipes and tubes to hustle in the energy they produce---that all involves very serious money.

But by combining tidal, current, wave, thermal and wind generating features at unusually productive spots, ocean co-generation becomes uniquely powerful.

Figuring that out was one of those "ah-ha!!" moments. It led to a new generation of multi-purpose co-generating off-shore arrays worthy of Rube Goldberg...or Rachel Carson.

For it was one thing to sink millions into a huge offshore array just for windmills. But in warmer waters (like Hawaii) the platforms can also harvest the temperature differential between the solar-heated water at the surface and those in the always-cold deep. With long tubing and simple heat exchangers, very cheap energy can be captured with these elegant passive units.

The ocean thermal devices can also be prohibitively expensive on a stand-alone basis. But combine them in synch with other sources, and a hugely profitable synergy emerges.

Indeed, the mainstay of Solartopian ocean energy has become these massive platforms that combine five green sources---wind, wave, tidal, current and ocean thermal. As such, they are balanced, stable, richly rewarding---and often immense---machines of mass delight.

All these technologies were separately known and operable at the dawn of the millennium. In the quarter-century since, there have been breakthroughs in each. There are abundant instances all over the world where each has profitably stood alone for many years now.

But they are all simple devices, and their collective success is no miracle. When they come together in these synergistic co-gen complexes, they are impressive to say the least.

Inevitably, solar panels blanket the platform superstructures.

Beneath the surface have come the bio-mass/algae farms and harvesters.

And then (as we'll see in a moment) there are the artificial reefs, with their fantastic food production.

Throw them all together and…voila!…you've got intriguing, intricate but gracefully functional power and protein machines that feed and move our new Solartopian millennium.

Today these green-co-generators have become virtual cities at sea. The energy, food and fresh water they produce are the essence of our post-pollution livelihood. The poisons they don't produce mean our species might survive even the global-warmed, reactor-irradiated aftermath of the Age of Fossil/Nuke.

Seafood & Scuba from the Solartopian Deep

While we're at it, let's talk more about those fish…and that algae.

These great green co-gen platforms that look so impressive, even from the air, do have giant underwater support structures. Massive legs must be punched deep into the ocean floor before they can tower high above the surface.

For years nobody really thought much about them. Until some clever Solartopian said: "Hey! Let's do fish!"

Indeed, the platforms are so big and so beautifully built that they have spawned a whole other dimension of extremely advanced bio-engineering and design, aimed at their undersides. The result is a bravura new world of "SolaReefs," a million cubic miles of exquisitely abundant estuaries.

The latest SolaReefs are utterly hypnotic in the density of their filaments and grace of their execution. Each new inauguration is a global news event, with dignitaries flocking from all over Solartopia, followed by the inevitable droves of eager tourists.

Where the waters are warm, the SolaReefs have created a wildly popular submarine-based tourist industry, complete with scuba schools and dive cults. Millions of Solartopian children of all ages have *ooohed* and *aaahed* at the startling sublimities of these underwater wonderlands.

The intricate, high-tech undersides of these sea-borne power stations have also spawned two more surprising offspring.

Algae Power and Sea Salad

Thanks to the carefully managed inputs of advanced hybrid nutrients, organically farmed algae plantations now "co-generate" a significant crop of bio-seamass for supplemental energy. Woven in and around the SolaReefs are a million miles of advanced bio-netting on which the algae thrives and multiplies. Among our health food advocates, this prolific, unstoppable weed of the sea supplies a whole range of precious vitamin and food supplements with a truly fanatic "algae-head" core market.

The algae is also a bio-fuel. There are hundreds of varieties. Some have epic energy value. Others have virtually none.

Just as happened above-ground with corn and soy, debate rages today over whether undersea algae should be fermented and burned for fuel, or preserved for food, or just left alone for the fish. Don't hold your breath until that one's resolved.

As for the ocean gourmet, the co-gen centers boast a booming crop of sea vegetables rising amidst the algae. From saltwater cucumbers to succulent sea weeds and an astounding cornucopia of underwater salad specialties, the bustling business of ocean gardening has introduced Solartopia to a whole new way of eating.

The art and science of open water aqua-culture has made these ever-evolving artificial reefs astonishingly fertile. The intricate substructures of these giant green generators spawn vital marine eco-systems that parallel the diversity of our coral reefs, now slowly recovering from the devastation of climate chaos and the relentless contamination of the Age of Fossil/Nuke.

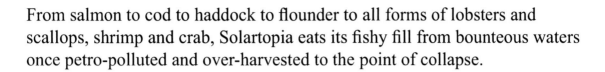

From salmon to cod to haddock to flounder to all forms of lobsters and scallops, shrimp and crab, Solartopia eats its fishy fill from bounteous waters once petro-polluted and over-harvested to the point of collapse.

Tourist subs and pleasure divers pick their way around Solartopia's gentle ocean power giants and their lush, bounteous SolaReefs. Thermal tubes and twirling turbines below, wave bobbers at the surface, booming windmills and shining PV panels above---they all combine to make these vital co-generators a joy to behold.

Working in diverse harmony, together and with our Earth, these icons of Solartopian synergy arrived just in time. Above all they say: we will find ways to survive... and we'll do it in style!

The Politics of Unpolluted Power

Not long into the new century, the unstoppable public demand for clean, green power became a crucial unifying factor for the European Union. Spurred by the irradiated, oil-soaked catastrophe of America's collapse, Europe in the new millennium raced to an amazingly prosperous renewable reality.

Spain, Italy, Belgium and Holland joined Germany and the Scandinavians in their wind-driven flight from nuke power.

Through their very aggressive Gamesa Corporation, the Spaniards exported a new "Armada" of windmills worldwide. Gamesa's prospectors scoured US wind sites from Ohio to the Great Plains, planting Spanish turbine towers like ancient flags of discovery.

With serendipity and prescience, innovation and desperation, the rest of Europe embraced Solartopian prosperity...but at varying speeds.

Left behind was France. Stuck with 55 calamitous *nukes de merde*, France's radioactive albatross saddled it with huge debt and an insanely expensive, shaky power grid.

Hooked on their decaying, decrepit reactors for some 80% of their electricity, the French eased gingerly toward the cheaper, cleaner renewables that made their neighbors so much richer and more secure.

Early in the new millennium, France abandoned all reactor construction. It desperately sought liberation from the *incroyable* burdens of radioactive waste and atomic debt. It was a dual liability for which France paid *tres cher* for decades.

In 2006, British Prime Minister Tony Blair attempted to revive atomic power. An angry chorus hooted him in as close to unison as this contentious isle ever gets. Even the most conservative Brits agreed that more failed reactor technology was as bad an idea as, say, attacking Iraq.

Today Great Britain is nuke free. It fairly bristles with wind turbines. Its towers bear paintings of everything from the Union Jack to adverts for the latest London plays and the third generation of Monty Python remakes. And the young men and women of its downsized military have never returned to the Middle East.

The Frozen Kuwait of H

Our H-airliner sails in silence past Norway, beyond the turbine-topped former oil derricks of the North Sea and into the North Atlantic. The "Green Maginot Line" of ocean co-generators stretches out to the south, far further than the eye can see. Its towering turbines spin in Solartopian synch past Spain and Gibraltar, Morocco and Nigeria, and all the way down to the tip of southern Africa.

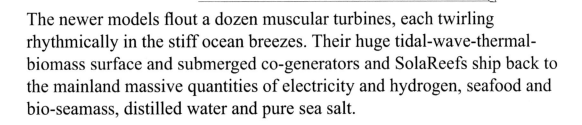

The newer models flout a dozen muscular turbines, each twirling rhythmically in the stiff ocean breezes. Their huge tidal-wave-thermal-biomass surface and submerged co-generators and SolaReefs ship back to the mainland massive quantities of electricity and hydrogen, seafood and bio-seamass, distilled water and pure sea salt.

Other windmills, far smaller, are perched atop dry old drilling rigs. They churn out clean electricity where once they spewed tar and CO_2, petro-filth and climate chaos.

To our right, we see Iceland. Its stark sub-Arctic ice-scape is a stunning reminder of how close we came to global demise.

At the turn of the millennium, this tiny nation was engulfed in environmental chaos. Its economy was nearly broken by absurdly expensive fossil fuel imports and the insidious impacts of climate catastrophe.

The response was dramatic: Reykjavik announced the first Solartopian conversion to 100% green energy. Its target date to be fossil/nuke-free was 2020.

That, Iceland easily beat.

Like Norway, this frigid isle has powerful water ways capable of producing almost unlimited hydropower. Iceland is also legend for its geothermal bounty. Its countless geysers and super-hot cauldrons overflow with up-wellings from the earth's core. Between its hot springs and water wheels, breezes and currents, Solartopian technologies let Iceland produce all the free hydrogen, electricity and geothermal heat it could ever need.

Ahead of schedule and under budget, the "Frozen Kuwait of H" raced Denmark and Norway to the zero fossil/nuke finish line in a dead heat.

The Icelanders then put their formidable fishing armada, their modest fleet of trucks and buses, trolleys and cars, and nearly all their industry deep into the brave renewable world of Solartopian energy.

With fuel cells and PV, with hybrid bio-fuels and hydrogen, with geothermal conversion and ever-more advanced green technologies, tiny Iceland became a super-efficient energy exporter---and very, very rich.

The same, unfortunately, could not be said for the United States.

Escape from Global Wierding

Flying in our quiet green-powered H-airliner, it's sometimes hard to remember that long before the Apocalyptic end of the Age of Fossil/Nuke, humankind had all the tools it needed to install a Solartopia. But King CONG said "NO!!"

The resistance was centered in the United States.

Ecologically and economically, humankind was beyond desperate. Fossil-fired carbon dioxide catastrophically unbalanced planetary weather patterns. Falsely termed "global warming," soaring CO_2 made for uncontrolled, unpredictable climate chaos. Simply put: the weather went stark raving mad. Energy expert Amory Lovins correctly called it "global wierding."

Here temperatures soared. There came horrific cold spells. Here there were devastating droughts. There came catastrophic flooding. Here species went extinct. There they (especially the insects) exploded out of control.

Cumulative heat creep melted the polar ice caps. Entire islands disappeared. Florida and the Gulf of Mexico were hammered again and again and yet again and then again by one "storm of the century" after another. The weather service ran out of names for hurricanes.

Low lying cities like New Orleans and Venice barely kept their heads above water. Then Katrina drowned the Big Easy in executive incompetence. After 2005, things only got worse.

Superheated oceans fed ever-stronger monsoons. Hurricanes and tsunamis stopped making the news. Tropical diseases like West Nile virus and avian flu rampaged through formerly frigid terrain. Malaria made its way to Montana and Mongolia.

Oil spills poisoned the seas and coated the beaches. Marine species disappeared in droves. Robins turned up in the Arctic. The Great Plains spun wildly from drought to flood and back again. Locusts became the national bird. The oceans went eco-mad.

Toxic clouds from gas and oil made lung disease a universal epidemic. Mountaintops were blown apart to get coal.

Atomic reactors succumbed to the quadruple whammy of terror attack, corporate greed, operational incompetence and structural impossibility. Simple decay rendered them inoperable. Disaster followed disaster. Chernobyl was dwarfed by the March of the Melt-Downs.

Would humankind survive? It was a close call, to say the least.

Too Cheap to Matter

In the wake of World War Two, President Harry Truman wanted to know about America's energy future. So he handed William Paley, chair of the Columbia Broadcast System, a Blue Ribbon Commission.

In 1952, Paley reported back: America's energy should come from the sun. The US would have 13 million solar-heated homes by 1975. Renewables would power a whole new level of American prosperity.

The seeds of Solartopia were ready to plant.

But a year later, Dwight Eisenhower steered the nation toward disaster.

In 1953 the Republican president left the solar option in the radioactive dust. He proclaimed that the "Peaceful Atom" would be the world's new energy miracle. Lewis Strauss, Chairman of the Atomic Energy Commission, said nuke power would be "too cheap to meter."

At least a half-trillion dollars in taxpayer handouts and sunk capital then poured into the most expensive technological failure in human history. All these years later, Solartopians find it hard to believe the decision to go nuke was ever seriously considered, let alone made.

Simply put: atomic power could never be made safe. Nor could it be made profitable or ecological.

It all started with huge government subsidies and the 1957 Price-Anderson Act, which protected reactor owners from major liability. Billions were invested. Scores of reactors went on line.

When push came to shove, the plants simply did not deliver. The bottom line was a downward spiral.

By the 1970s, the industry crashed into a bottomless financial, political and technical quagmire. All US reactor orders placed after 1974 were cancelled.

The Paley Report's pro-solar spirit was reborn in 1976. With the US wasting half the energy it burned, Amory Lovins wrote in *Foreign Affairs* of a "Road Not Taken" based on increased efficiency and conservation. Ecologist Barry Commoner, in the *Politics of Energy*, proposed a Solartopian future. Natural gas would be the bridge to wind power, renewable designs and methane production from energy crops and composted urban waste.

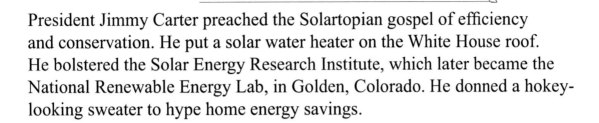

President Jimmy Carter preached the Solartopian gospel of efficiency and conservation. He put a solar water heater on the White House roof. He bolstered the Solar Energy Research Institute, which later became the National Renewable Energy Lab, in Golden, Colorado. He donned a hokey-looking sweater to hype home energy savings.

Then he dumped countless billions into the doomed, dirty technology of oil shale. He waffled on nuke power at Seabrook, New Hampshire, and other reactor sites, where mass demonstrations erupted, complete with thousands of non-violent arrests among those who were otherwise his strongest supporters. He failed to protect the embryonic renewables industry from the mega-rich King CONG petro-right.

Then he punched into a tar-baby---the hostage crisis in oil-rich Iran from which his presidency never got free.

The Reagan Regression

Solartopian America sprouted its first serious grass roots in the Golden State. Governor Jerry Brown used tax credits to erect some 17,000 early turbines. At Livermore and Palm Springs, enough wind-drive electricity was harvested to power San Francisco, and more.

In the Mojave desert, nine big trough mirror arrays converted the sun into cheap electricity. A solar power tower rose like a giant candle out of the sands near Needles, shining a blinding white light a hundred feet in the air.

Photovoltaic panels began converting the sun's energy directly into usable home-based electricity.

Across America, Solartopia beckoned like a new gold rush. "Green geek" entrepreneurs went prospecting in the solar/wind future from their 1970s garages and backyards in parallel rhythm with the computer geeks next door.

In the Carter '70s, the solar juggernaut seemed poised to net America trillions. The global transformation would guarantee a permanent green prosperity. The foreign and domestic eco-markets promised the ultimate US cash cow.

Until…Ronald Reagan.

The Gipper had made his name working for General Electric, which was bullish on both nuke weapons and nuke power.

As president, Reagan paid them back with an Ike re-run. He ripped Carter's money-saving solar panels off the White House roof. He gutted federal renewables research. He canceled green tax credits. He drove the dazed solar business, with some 10,000 American employees, straight to Death Valley.

In California, Republican Governor George Deukmejian followed Jerry Brown, and did the same thing. For the second time in US history, Solartopia was stillborn at the brink. The green factories shut. The solar jobs evaporated. Reagan and his Texas oil Vice President George H.W. Bush revived the fossil/nuke nightmare.

In the United States (unlike in Europe and Japan) renewable energy shriveled and starved. But it did not die.

The PV Revolution Reborn

With the 1992 election of Bill Clinton came a feeble solar revival. In Elvis-like spurts, he sustained a Solartopian façade. But he never addressed the gap between hype and performance.

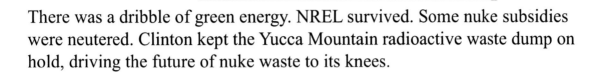

There was a dribble of green energy. NREL survived. Some nuke subsidies were neutered. Clinton kept the Yucca Mountain radioactive waste dump on hold, driving the future of nuke waste to its knees.

He promised "a million solar rooftops," but delivered far fewer. (In fact, he failed even to restore Jimmy Carter's solar panels to his own roof at the White House.) He brought no Paley-style penetration for a renewable industry that could have re-energized American green leadership in the world.

By all rights, the revolution in solar energy should have paralleled the one in personal computers and the internet.

But while the www and PC boomed in the US, the action in wind power went to Europe. Annual global growth rates of installed wind capacity soared to 25% and more. The Danes and Germans made the big money. What might have been a trillion job-creating US dollars became Euros instead. As for photovoltaics, Germany, Japan and Israel took the gold.

PV was the legitimate child of the US space program. The first solar cells were born in the early 1950s at Bell Labs. They helped power the Vanguard satellite. (Eighty years later, those very cells still generate electricity. If there's a theoretical limit to the PV life span, as of A.D. 2030, we've yet to see it).

When Ike went nuclear, America's solar industry was plunged into a hardscrabble struggle to stay alive. It scraped by on the millions of tiny cells installed in watches and calculators.

But when it came time to really cash in, the big money went to Sanyo and Sharp, Kyocera and Siemens.

PV became a gargantuan global cash cow. Its American inventor was left sucking the silicon dust---while still paying in blood and treasure for endless, futile wars for oil.

The Age of Enron

In 2002, Jeremy Rifkin's *Hydrogen Economy* argued that H would
power a global economy controlled at the grassroots. It would be clean,
decentralized, efficient and infinite. It would end the King CONG nightmare.

But the first eight years of the new millennium were mired in economic
chaos, military disaster, ecological ruin, epic incompetence, constitutional
catastrophe, political authoritarianism and astonishing corruption.

Calling it the Age of Enron, some historians compare those years to the
delerium tremens of a dry drunk. Others liken them to the violent shakes of
hopeless addict, tragically trapped by heroin or nicotine, sugar or television-
--or, more to the point, fossil and nuclear fuels, and the corporate cash they
funneled to petro-nuke politicians.

By the time America staggered through the Enron collapse, the high ground
in wind, PV and H technologies was firmly in foreign hands.

The poisoned and polluted US had repeated its economic and ecological
follies as tragedy and farce.

In the 1970s and 1980s, Detroit scoffed at energy efficient automobiles.
So Honda and Toyota built factories in the US to make their gas-sipping
Civics and smoothly efficient Corollas. They reaped huge profits and killed
Chrysler.

In the early 2000s, fossil addiction crippled the US yet again. Ford and the
rest of Detroit this time talked a good green game. But Toyota and Honda
made the actual cars, this time hybrids.

So Detroit died again. GM and Ford were buried by the Japanese where
Chrysler had expired before. Even the production of mass transit---the
booming Solartopian train and trolley revival---went to Europe... and China.

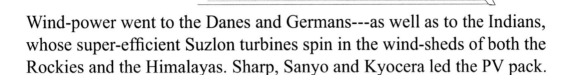

Wind-power went to the Danes and Germans---as well as to the Indians, whose super-efficient Suzlon turbines spin in the wind-sheds of both the Rockies and the Himalayas. Sharp, Sanyo and Kyocera led the PV pack.

By the time the US got out of the Bushes and into the Solartopian sun, the renewable technologies it had pioneered were owned and operated overseas. The world's once-richest nation could barely afford the energy to keep itself alive. The jobs that could have been American were now everywhere but. While US troops killed and died for oil, the green energy future slipped away.

The World Trade Center was a memory. New Orleans was drowned and poisoned. Gasoline prices soared. There was no mass transit. The Constitution was in tatters. The deficits were staggering, the gargantuan debt foreign-owned. And still, all the real money went to war…and oil.

Amidst the wreckage, the idea and ideals of Solartopia became a shining beacon of hope… and hype.

Even the corporations began talking up green energy. With the country broke and in shock, the American grass roots finally took a good look at the numbers… and the carnage… and realized that green power was a necessary inevitability.

But actually getting from King CONG to Solartopia would be very much another story.

The Murder of Mass Transit

The American coast is at last in sight! As we begin our light lunch of sun-baked sea food and ocean vegetables, we see another mega-phalanx of turbine towers and co-gen centers stretching parallel to the ones we left behind off Europe and Africa.

From Nova Scotia to Argentina, the Great American Array stands tall amidst the endless waves and currents, gusts and tides of the mighty Atlantic.

Below the surface, these massive machines feed the spectacular undersea web of tubes and wires that move electricity and hydrogen into America's coastal megalopolis.

The on-shore use of off-shore protons and electrons now helps power---pollution free---America's redesigned, ultra-efficient public transportation system.

Incredibly, its predecessor was once murdered in cold corporate blood.

Time was, Americans could board the MTA in Boston and ride one trolley system to the next all the way to St. Louis. In Los Angeles and other cities of the west, one could travel from desert to ocean, mountains to valley, just by jumping from one trolley to the next.

Americans loved riding their clean, safe, efficient rail system. As late as 1920 just one US family in ten owned an automobile. And that was the heinous motive in what we now call "the eco-crime of the 20th Century."

To invent America's "love affair" with the automobile, General Motors and its cohort gas, glass, rubber and banking conspirators, set out to kill the competition. Over the course of three decades, they bought and buried what had been the world's greatest mass transit system.

Some eighty American cities lost their light rail. In its place came dirty, expensive and inefficient gas-driven buses---or nothing at all. As GM wanted, millions of Americans were forced to turn to private automobiles.

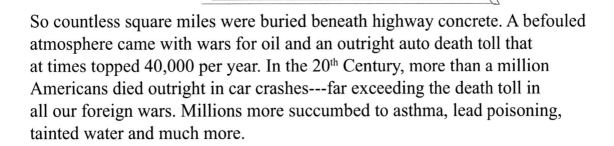

So countless square miles were buried beneath highway concrete. A befouled atmosphere came with wars for oil and an outright auto death toll that at times topped 40,000 per year. In the 20th Century, more than a million Americans died outright in car crashes---far exceeding the death toll in all our foreign wars. Millions more succumbed to asthma, lead poisoning, tainted water and much more.

Today Solartopian school children shake their heads in disbelief as they read how the King CONG corporations left a gridlocked nation at the mercy of the gas-fired automobile. That much-hyped "love affair" was a shotgun wedding. Our beloved first spouse---rail travel---had been blasted dead.

At the Solartopian dawn, America was a nation held hostage, a hamstrung oil addict, unable to compete in world markets. With their modernized mass transit systems, Europe and Japan left the US behind.

Finally freeing ourselves from the automobile was as painful and expensive as any domestic divorce. Reconstructing the modern re-incarnation of what was once the world's great mass transit system was one of the great green accomplishments of the Solartopian Age.

Today, our hyper-efficient, bio-fueled, solar-paneled passenger trains and sleek, sweet urban trolleys have freed the US from Big Oil's double death grip. A nation now free to move around has regained its place as a credible player in the world economy.

But we still pay a fearsome price.

The Sprawlburbian Corpse

The automobile also stuck Solartopia with the curse of sprawlburbia.

In those rare instances where developers actually paid attention to the natural environment, a few livable housing developments did emerge from 20th Century. But by and large, from sea to sea, rank, raunchy, retrograde suburbs infested the American countryside like a terminal cancer.

Beginning with Levittown just after World War 2, these soul-less mass housing messes turned a billion American acres into dilapidated eco-trash. Uncaring speculators and their lackey zoning boards ripped out the heart of America's forests, fields and farmland. They injected into the eco-sphere a horrific virus of shoddy, over-priced sprawlshacks that poisoned us all.

Last century's suburbs were the automobile's mutant twin. They offered millions of American families a chance to own a home. Where they were well-built, and the trees were left to grow, they could offer a decent life.

But most made Americans lonely slaves to the auto culture. The barren, isolated tracts were often deeply alienating and depressing. At war with nature and community, the endless, faceless ticky-tacky had no human or natural soul or center.

Once infected, there was no stopping the spread of cheap, eco-deadly, utterly mindless anti-architecture. Zoning boards everywhere rubber stamped variances that allowed the destruction of America's most vital greenspace.

And suburban developers never seemed to grasp---or care about---the fact that in the northern hemisphere, energy and light come through windows on the south. Fuel can be saved by insulating rooftops and north walls.

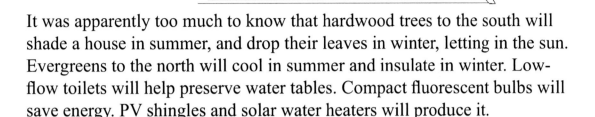

It was apparently too much to know that hardwood trees to the south will shade a house in summer, and drop their leaves in winter, letting in the sun. Evergreens to the north will cool in summer and insulate in winter. Low-flow toilets will help preserve water tables. Compact fluorescent bulbs will save energy. PV shingles and solar water heaters will produce it.

Plastic PVC components, on the other hand, spew toxic poisons, killing firefighters and permanently polluting the land. Paving eco-systems, leveling forests and draining wetlands for throw-away dwellings yielded short-term corporate profits. But long-term social disaster proved a dead certainty.

Early in the new millennium, sprawlburbia imploded. Even those big, fancy "McMansions" succumbed to mould and collapse.

With the horrible loss of life and drop in fertility that accompanied global warming and the March of the Melt-Downs, the housing bubble burst. Car commuting became a financial sinkhole and a gridlocked impossibility. Urban mass transit could not be revived fast enough. Remote, unreachable, unsustainable American suburbs died in droves.

Solartopia is now littered with countless abandoned housing and commercial developments. Most simply rot. Trees sprout up where nature reclaims its own. Vines and flowers punch their way through concrete driveways. Shrubs and vines chew the plywood, pulling it back to earth.

Many of these trashy relics have been reclaimed by a new generation of "sprawl squatters." To them, the bizarre concept of the "lawn"---a captive square of useless genetically-modified grass---has grown progressively more incomprehensible. The lunacy of installing, spraying and artificially fertilizing this useless anti-crop remains a case study in eco-cide.

In Solartopia, countless abandoned lawns have been transformed into organic gardens. Food, fuel and flowers bloom where once there was a virtual green desert. Every inch of sprawlburbia within our economic and technical grasp has been or soon will be reclaimed, revamped and replanted.

Every one of those sad sprawlshacks will either be dismantled and recycled, or solarized and made sufficiently efficient to survive the post-auto era. When the very last sprawlburb is fully converted to a self-sustainable community, a national holiday will be declared. Then we'll know Solartopia has truly come of age.

Solar Solar New York New York

Along the coasts, America's hybridized public transit system is powered in part with mega offshore co-generation centers like the ones we just saw down there along the George's Bank. The output is matched on shore by billions of PV cells. They cover every Solartopian rooftop and south face, not to mention the composite skin of all our vehicles, from the wings of this H-airliner to the hoods of our hypercars.

Stringent codes pioneered in Europe have long since required that all US homes, office buildings and public places be made or retro-fitted with roofing materials and glass panes embedding PV. Solar hot water heaters are mandatory. Many are hidden amidst the crops and shrubs of our gorgeous rooftop gardens.

The US suffered horrific economic and ecological pain on the way here. That old monster movie showing King CONG attacking the NY subway system, then howling astride the Empire State Building, was not just cinematic hype. It was the corporate reality of Coal, Oil, Nukes and Gas.

But CONG's iron grip meant certain economic and ecological death. So, kicking and screaming, America found its way to Solartopia.

New York went first.

As we approach the "Big Green Apple," the solar panels erected at the sacred site of the downed World Trade Center gleam in the noonday sun.

For years after 9/11, endless bickering blighted the future of the stricken WTC lot. What finally rose from the ashes pleases everyone… and no one.

On one thing all do agree---the reborn WTC must always host a working PV array… an "eternal solar light"…even if it had to be retrofitted after the fact. Those who truly love New York above all want it kept free from the petro/ nuke-addiction that funded the murder of so many Americans on that awful day.

In their honor, the city requires that all buildings, old and new, must be rendered ultra-efficient. They must be heated and cooled at least in part by geothermal wells. PV and fuel cells are also obligatory. And every building must be self-contained. Its wastes are recycled for energy. All usable organic matter goes to parks and gardens inside the city, or to the greenbelt just beyond.

Geothermal was easy. As early as 2003, Manhattan began to use deep geothermal drilling as part of the energy mix.

Just a few feet down, the earth's crust can be a steady year-round 55 degrees. So a geothermal well can cool in the summer and heat in the winter. As the earth balances our buildings' base temperature, it saves huge quantities of energy.

New York makes all new structures follow the lead of the landmark Citicorp tower, whose signature slanted south-facing rooftop is carpeted with PV. Like hundreds of other older buildings, the southern walls are covered with solar collectors, slashing Citicorp's energy appetite---and its utility bills.

Urban solar took off around 2006 and never looked back. *Solaire*, the first totally solar urban housing development, opened at Battery Park City, hallowed site of the pioneer Solartopian "No Nukes" Concerts.

They were staged by Musicians United for Safe Energy (MUSE) soon after the 1979 Three Mile Island disaster inaugurated the March of the Melt-Downs. One outdoor gathering drew 200,000 people. Rock legends Bruce Springsteen, Bonnie Raitt, Jackson Browne, CSN, Carly Simon, James Taylor and many more, sang to the coming of Solartopia. As *Solaire* opened a quarter-century later, one of the MUSE organizers, John Hall, began a stellar Solartopian career in the US Congress. Among other things, he helped shut the reactors at Indian Point, 45 miles north of Battery Park City.

Today *Solaire* is preserved as a national monument. It features a modest museum honoring America's pioneer anti-nuke movement, highlighted by video from the concert.

Like every other structure in New York, the museum is covered with the latest generation of composite lenses that focus sunlight on tiny points of silicon. With them, a bare fraction of Earth's sunlight can now power our great cities, whose efficiency keeps soaring. Sun-powered roofing shingles, siding and windowpanes are everywhere. Embedding glass, paint and all forms of building materials with solar capacity is a national pastime.

Beneath the streets, New York and its urban American siblings host a labyrinth of hydrogen piping and electric cabling. The Great American H-Net is fed by offshore and PV generators. It backs up those parts of the post-industrial infrastructure that need supplemental juice. It helps feed countless fuel cells that can power homes and office towers, cars and buses, intra-urban light rail and long-distance passenger trains.

In Central Park, a working Dutch-style windmill commemorates North America's first, erected in the 1660s, when the city was still New Amsterdam.

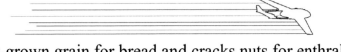

Today it grinds locally-grown grain for bread and cracks nuts for enthralled toddlers. It's a fitting monument to a society that that no longer sends its young to war in search of energy, and need not fear attack from oil-funded terrorists.

Offal Good

Drowning in their own sewage, cities like New York desperately embraced the biggest public works project since the conversion of the interstate highway system.

Sewage systems everywhere double as energy-generating compost operations. Natural aerobic and anaerobic digestion, algae generation, microbiological biomass decomposition and much more have created the trillion-dollar business of converting waste to power.

Few today can comprehend it… it's hard to even say it now… but this country once actually dumped its human wastes onto the land and into the oceans!

Now every city in the US, every suburb, every farm, every factory, every individual building, by law, hosts a high-powered waste digester.

Many Americans carefully preserve their personal bio-fuel for home and office. Millions consider it an act of "structural patriotism" to time their bodily functions for the buildings they want to power. Some greedy businesses now try to demand a certain "contribution" as a condition of employment. We expect this will be ruled unConstitutional (no pun intended).

Pay toilets dispense cash paybacks to those who use them. Their technical name is Compensated Human Biomass Depositories. Some of the sillier cities have dubbed them "Chubdies."

Your average Solartopian just calls them they've always been called. But the days of "flush and forget" are long gone. The calculated guidance of this most basic bodily function is now an act of personal pride.

Power from the Farms and Swamps

Other bio-sources are equally emblematic. In the late 1900s, agri-giants like Archer-Daniels-Midland pushed ethanol, the alcohol fuel based on corn. Soy diesel powered the mainstream. Used restaurant cooking oil became a hot commodity.

Solartopian heroes like Bonnie Raitt and Willie Nelson made history using soy diesel and ethanol to power their tour buses. Bonnie's "Green Highways" campaign, and "Bio-Willie's" soy diesel (along with their music, which is as popular as ever) earned them eco-sainthood in the Solartopian pantheon.

As soy and corn paved the way for the bio-fuels revolution, bitter controversy arose over the use of land and resources that were needed for food. In some cases, previously untouched forests were leveled by the demand for energy crops, as they had been for decades with the spread of beef production.

Early Solartopians responded with a largely successful global campaign to make bio-fuels truly sustainable. But it's still a struggle. As with all things on this Earth, the balance between individual economic gain and common ecological reality is a source of constant contention.

So corn and soy have long since been replaced as energy crops by the far more efficient "incredible in-edibles." Switchgrass, hemp, miscanthus, poplar trees, algae, kudzu are cheap and easy to grow. As sustainable perennials, these extremely profitable cash crops have helped save countless family farms and (along with wind power) much of rural America.

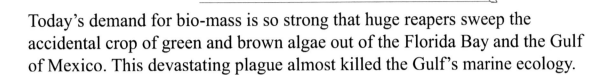

Today's demand for bio-mass is so strong that huge reapers sweep the accidental crop of green and brown algae out of the Florida Bay and the Gulf of Mexico. This devastating plague almost killed the Gulf's marine ecology.

Out in these semi-tropical waters, the algae blocked the sun, then dropped to the Gulf and Bay bottom, sucking the oxygen out of the water and all but killing one of the world's great estuaries.

This same algae now helps power Miami, Tampa, Pensacola, Galveston, Houston. It is harvested at great profit, lifting the Gulf from its death bed.

Along the way, Big Sugar has been booted out of the Everglades, where its federally subsidized dumping of fertilizers and disruption of water flow all but killed the eco-system. Sugar is now grown in places more appropriate, both for sweetener and for fuel. The south Florida bio-region has revived. It teems with the marine life once nearly extinguished by the lethal leavings of King CONG's corporate cousin.

Sugar, of course, also has a long bio-fuel history. Far to our south, Brazil and Cuba have pioneered the use of fermented cane stalks as a major fuel source. Way back in the 20th Century, the Brazilians made news by converting much of their auto fleet to alcohol and ethanol from their sweetest crop.

In the Amazon, fights still rage to protect Earth's few remaining virgin eco-systems from the pursuit of ever-more fuel crops. But for the Cubans, the key has been a total conversion to organic farming. Under Fidel I, the American embargo, and the collapse of their patron Soviet Union, cut off the option of chemical agriculture. Ironically, because the island has been "deprived" for so long, Cuban produce is prized the world over for its nutritional purity and organic richness.

Ninety miles to Cuba's north, of all the American dead zones brought improbably back to life, none seem more miraculous than the post-pollution Everglades "River of Grass" and Florida Bay.

Simply put: they are reborn as the incredibly fertile eco-systems they were meant to be.

Every day the mighty alligator and tremendous tarpon, once both on the brink of extinction, thrill thousands of admirers. Named for the legendary environmentalists who helped save them, the "George & Mary Barley Eco-Tours" draw green trekkers from all over the world.

They ride the bio-fueled airboats and canoe the exquisite by-ways of this sub-tropical Solartopian paradise. And they always come back for more.

Bio-Fuels for the Masses...from the Trashes

Conversely, methane wafting up from rotting garbage dumps has also turned to green gold. While they last, America's waste heaps are a rich Solartopian gas mine.

But with the triumph of universal recycling and total efficiency, the waste stream---like our petroleum supply before it---is drying up. The ancient dumps are almost drained of their methane. Green derricks have sucked dry nearly every trash heap in America.

Some of even the most toxic of all the landfills are now restored to field, forest and wetland. It's really nice, you know, to fly over and feast our eyes on deep living green, where once there was deathly filth.

It's even fun, sometimes, to watch our kids' eyes roll as we rant on about the beauties of depleted waste dumps.

When it comes to the gap between the generations, some things will never change, even in the brave new renewable world of Solartopian energy.

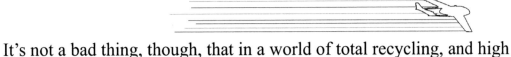

It's not a bad thing, though, that in a world of total recycling, and high premiums for natural methane, our kids will grow up barely remembering the absurd phenomenon we once called "waste dumps."

Will they be missed? We don't think so!

On the Green Mend

But for those of us who remember, Solartopia got real in a hellish mega-drama. We spent every ounce of our political strength to get this far. It took oil wars, climate catastrophes, melt-downs, would-be dictatorships, ghastly pollution plagues, financial collapse and too much more to finally force effective action. We almost lost our planet, our rights, our government, our freedom, our ability to reproduce, you name it.

In retrospect, getting to Solartopia was impossible. It could not have happened.

But hey!....somehow...we did it.

The mass marches, the internet, the desperate struggles to save the Bill of Rights, the global campaigns for peace, the astounding incompetence of the King CONG presidencies, the collapse of the petro-dictatorships, the dismantling of the multi-national corporations, the slow but steady economic, political and spiritual spread of the Great Green Gospel--- somehow, they all came together to make a revolution without which humankind could not have survived.

When fossil fuels and nuclear power were finally banned, petro-terrorism starved. And so did King CONG.

Saudi Arabia did not quite revert to its 1930s status as the world's poorest per capita nation. But it downscaled to an income based on the last best use of petroleum---for medicinal purposes.

The oil barons of Texas did not exactly disappear. But their reins of power did go the way of the dinosaurs that gave us oil in the first place.

The maturing Solartopian millennium has pushed petroleum almost entirely out of the fuel market. In the third decade of the 21st Century, it has reverted to its first use in the 19th---as "snake oil." What slender prices oil commands today come through pharmaceutical and exotic chemical applications.

Today's addictions to oil have nothing to do with powering cars. Or terror attacks. Or as a justification for war.

On the other hand, if you have a stomach ache, or need an exotic remedy, then by all means---give your separate thanks for that bilious black ooze that has caused us all so much grief, but can provide occasional digestive relief.

Into the Solartopian West

Against all previous odds, New York's air sparkles clean like Copenhagen's. Where it was once thick with smog, we can now see the Solartopian wind farms that dot the high ridges of the Catskills and Alleghenies.

As we fly west into the rich Pennsylvania heartland, we approach the still-hot reactors at Three Mile Island. They form a permanent monument to the radioactive arrogance for which we still pay such a fearsome price---and have zero tolerance.

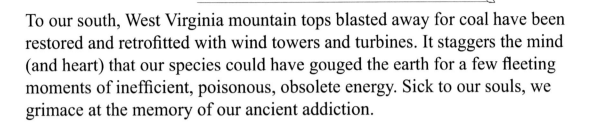

To our south, West Virginia mountain tops blasted away for coal have been restored and retrofitted with wind towers and turbines. It staggers the mind (and heart) that our species could have gouged the earth for a few fleeting moments of inefficient, poisonous, obsolete energy. Sick to our souls, we grimace at the memory of our ancient addiction.

On our right, along the Great Lakes, a string of windmills grace Buffalo's bustling shoreline and inland ridges. Primitive by today's standards, these were installed just after Toronto's and Cleveland's in the fast march of turbines and towers plunked down along America's inland sea.

Out in its midst is the Great Lakes Array that blew open American's hydro-wind heartland. They may lack the brute strength of their ocean kin. But Lakes Huron, Erie, Michigan, Ontario and Superior are all seriously wind-swept within five miles of shore.

One by one, the cities of Windsor, London, Toronto, Buffalo, Erie, Cleveland, Toledo, Detroit, Gary, Chicago, Milwaukee and Duluth built very big platforms in the fresh, relatively shallow waters near their city centers. Rising out of those once filthy waters, the turbines send clean, very cheap electricity into post-industrial cities once all but consigned to the "rust belt" scrap heap.

At the dawn of the 20th Century, it was cheap juice from Niagara Falls that lit Buffalo's first boom.

At the dawn of the 21st, at the Solartopian sunrise, the endless electron flow from those huge "Lake Effect" wind turbines blew that rust off the midwest and propelled it into a powerful new age of eco-prosperity.

This surging flow of offshore H and wind-driven electricity has made urban self-sufficiency just a Solartopian *ho-hum*. The countless thousands of jobs created and sustained are deeply embedded in the American heartland.

The greenspace of every lakefront downtown invariably hosts a public telescope. They lovingly scan the massive offshore turbines that produce so much power. They all bear the same inscription:

Remember 9/11/2001… Honor New Orleans…No More King CONG.

Four Built in O-HI-O

As we pass over the Mighty Buckeye Turbine Fields, we can spot Ohio's pioneer windmills at Bowling Green.

In September, 2004, BG's municipal-owned utility installed two Vestas machines. At 1.8 megawatts and 500 feet from tip to ground, they now seem virtual miniatures.

But they belong to the public, Sacramento-style. When numbers three and four came on line in 2005, they opened Ohio to its golden age of towering turbines.

Ohio is comparatively breeze-challenged. But hyper-efficient turbines, a great grid, limited sunlight and endless urban demand have made this an unlikely wind Mecca.

Once in dire straits, Ohio was desperate to escape the fossil/nuke grip. Its first major battle came in Cleveland, where young Mayor Dennis Kucinich barely managed to save the Municipal Light System, which was established in 1914. Cleveland bankers wanted it dead, but Kucinich protected the Muni, which later helped move the state to green power. (Kucinich's long Solartopian career in the US House is most frequently remembered for his work in establishing a federal Department of Peace).

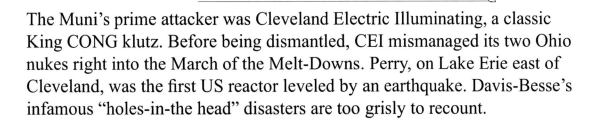

The Muni's prime attacker was Cleveland Electric Illuminating, a classic King CONG klutz. Before being dismantled, CEI mismanaged its two Ohio nukes right into the March of the Melt-Downs. Perry, on Lake Erie east of Cleveland, was the first US reactor leveled by an earthquake. Davis-Besse's infamous "holes-in-the head" disasters are too grisly to recount.

Imperious, impenetrable and supremely incompetent, CEI's offspring never mastered the gargantuan service territory to which they kept greedily annexing more. They plunged their customers into darkness, then crashed and burned.

Today, every former CEI asset is municipally owned. Every Ohio turbine beats with the clean, reliable heart of public green power. They are object lessons in the grassroots revolution that has remade the way Solartopia gets its electricity.

Back Home Again, In Windiana

In the early midwestern afternoon, our H-airliner soars past the giant pinwheels that power the Windy City. The gorgeous shoreline of this "Breeze Butcher to the World" bristles with the tremendous turbines that power its Solartopian prosperity.

Then we angle across the Mississippi and into the great Windiana heartland.

In the 1970s, the visionary William Heronemus dubbed the land between the Mississippi and the Rockies the "Saudi Arabia of Wind." That was when the Saudis were super-rich, using their ill-got oily booty to fund terror and buy the politicians that let it happen.

Gratefully, the Saudis are long since broke. And the native Americans of the prairie, once desperately impoverished, now reap a rich renewable harvest from the powerful spirits that blow across their lands.

In their honor, a new name has stuck to this bio-region of Solartopian bounty: "Windiana".

Today's forever flat, ever-blustery American prairie is thickly sprouted, as far as the eye can see, with tens of thousands of wind turbines. Most are in the 2.5-3.0 megawatt range.

At 200-300 feet high, these "prairie pinwheels" are tiny compared with the giant off-shore rigs that power the coastal and lakeside cities. But there are so many of them it can stagger the eye.

Most Solartopians (especially the youngsters) simply accept these turbines and towers as a deep-rooted feature of the natural landscape. They've "always been there," they say. "What's the Big Deal?"

If only they knew…!

C-BED to the Rescue

Some of these "combines in the sky" were originally developed by predatory speculators and corporate "windcatters" plenty eager---as always---to cheat the locals for a quick buck.

But then the farmers fought back through "Community-Based Energy Development (C-BED)" and some serious organizing.

On April 29, 1994, an anti-nuke coalition forced the Minnesota legislature to mandate the Northern States Power utility to buy 400 megawatts of wind.

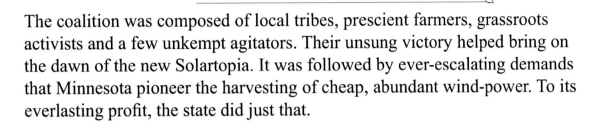

The coalition was composed of local tribes, prescient farmers, grassroots activists and a few unkempt agitators. Their unsung victory helped bring on the dawn of the new Solartopia. It was followed by ever-escalating demands that Minnesota pioneer the harvesting of cheap, abundant wind-power. To its everlasting profit, the state did just that.

Hidden in the mix was a Solartopian pioneer named Dan Juhl. Helping build the industry from the ground up, Juhl installed his own utility-scale turbine farm at Woodstock, Minnesota (home of the annual "Windstock" music festival).

Juhl pioneered America's early model of farmer/community turbine ownership. These "Family Juhls" are the neighborly coops and family eco-ventures that anchor Solartopia deep in the Great Plains community. Mirroring the original Danish model of community ownership, the American farmer/community-owned wind harvest has preserved thousands of family homestead. It helps draw countless young people back to the Great Plains, which were virtually depopulated as the millennium dawned.

Windiana has saved the health and productivity of millions of acres of precious land, without whose regenerative powers we might have lost this planet---not to mention the ability to feed ourselves.

Some oldtimers (and even their kids) still say the turbines are un-scenic eyesores. A lot of projects have been stopped along the way.

But for mainstream Solartopia, these prairie turbines are lively monuments to successful resource management and good communal sense. Windiana's cash crops are in the food and bio-fuels it grows on the ground, and in the air that moves above. Clutching those Family Juhls for all they're worth--- which has proven to be quite a lot--- grassland agriculture has survived and thrived.

(Our journal continues on page 75)

THE RANCHO SECO/PV ICON--- This photo of the dead Rancho Seco nuclear plant, surrounded by operating photovoltaic (PV) arrays remains one of the vital Solartopian icons. When the people of Sacramento voted the reactor shut in 1989, it actually did. The city's public-owned Sacramento Municipal Utility District (SMUD) began its great pioneer conversion to Solartopian power. Though extremely inefficient by today's standards, the PV cells surrounding the reactor corpse still generate electricity and are being continually studied to determine their true ultimate lifespan. Parts of the reactor are still dangerously radioactive.

THE FIRST FAMILY JUHL---The DanMar wind farm at Woodstock, Minnesota was the pioneer farmer-owned "Family Juhl." Built by Dan and Mary Juhl in the late 1990s, its 17 early Windiana Breeze Geezers broke wind for a whole new method of local energy ownership. The power contracts for it were made possible by a pioneer Solartopian anti-nuclear campaign that forced utilities to buy wind-generated electricity. Though its turbines are now considered tiny, this wind farm still generates power profitably. Now a national monument, this is the site of the annual "Windstock Music Festival."

THE FIRST SOLARTOPIAN CLOCK: This primal version of the wildly popular and increasingly sophisticated Solartopian Clock was first unveiled around Earth Day, 2007. A prestigious committee of global scientists, financiers, politicians and activists continues to monitor and evaluate the state of green power each year, and issues updates accordingly (copies of this first, primitive clock are now exceedingly rare).

Progress towards Solartopia came slowly through the first decade, but accelerated rapidly between 2017 and 2022, then hit warp speed as the renewable industry achieved saturation take-off. The personnel on the Calendar Committee has turned over often since 2007. But thousands of comments and conceptualizations still pour in to **www.solartopia.org**.

(Our journal continues from page 71)

Green Communal Windians

So, too, Native America.

Near the South Dakota town of St. Francis, a turbine owned by the Rosebud Sioux makes the point.

It was erected in 2003. It spins within miles of Wounded Knee, site of the infamous 1890 massacre that ended the first round of Indian resistance.

Over a century later, the 750-kilowatt Rosebud turbine inaugurated another era: the great Windian "gold rush in the sky."

Thousands of airborne combines now spin above "Windian Country," nearly all of them owned by tribes once deemed extinct. The initial few thousand native-owned megawatts were financed by casinos that poured billions into tribal coffers all over the US.

But gambling lost its edge when those nutty Baby Boomers finally gave way to a new generation of Solartopians. More interested in survival than shooting craps, their green-powered progeny joined the revived native communities in building a resilient network of wind, solar, biomass and geothermal assets that long ago out-earned the casinos.

From that single Rosebud turbine, the affiliated tribes of Windiana have achieved total energy self-sufficiency. They send trillions of kilowatts to market. They reap untold wealth, not least of which is a deepened sense of the natural harmony on which their communities were originally founded so many millennia ago.

The barren, remote reservations to which so many natives were cynically shunted have grown rich and comfortable. But they have also grown savvy in the ways of the government that so long tormented them.

The New Windians are a potent force in Solartopian America. They boast total energy self-sufficiency, extremely well-organized tribal governments, serious wealth and a powerful, focussed political arm. Taken in concert, the spread of farm/community and tribal ownership of wind power and other renewables have redefined the Solartopian power balance.

Hard as it is to believe, there was once a time when the renewable energy industry had but a tiny handful of financially vested advocates. It could not stand up to King CONG.

Today, the reverse is true. The native ghosts of Wounded Knee have returned, with a great green vengeance.

Long, Tall Lingerie

As we fly quietly over the gentle hills and fertile fields of rural Kansas, we can see the source of some unexpected income that has come to wind farmers. Let's just say it's "non-traditional."

The tall turbine towers that once stood so staid and stately now feed a wildly popular NCAA event---Windiana's annual "decorate your big pole" contest. Every year plains farmers lease out a few hundred towers to be redecorated by college students. Big money goes to the winners---as long as they keep it decent.

Some owners have gone even further. They're cashing in on well-paid "tall-vertisements" or "tower-ads."

Some of them are ...shall we say…. "evocative." Like those endless battles over decorating offshore wave worms, communal debate on the popular aesthetics of tower design rages everywhere.

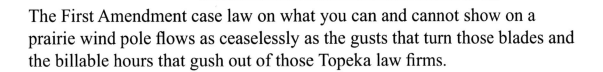

The First Amendment case law on what you can and cannot show on a prairie wind pole flows as ceaselessly as the gusts that turn those blades and the billable hours that gush out of those Topeka law firms.

Of course the hue and cry has helped turn the "lingerie section" of northeast Kansas into Windiana's biggest tourist draw.

In fact, wherever you go on today's American prairie, the staid, stately all-white turbine towers of times gone by have been gussied up in ways guaranteed to provoke Paul Bunyan's wildest fantasies.

To travel through some of today's wind farms is to wonder who's running the madhouse. It's just not your grandfather's train ride across the country any more. And for that, we are grateful.

Painted or otherwise, these giant windmills have revived a farm community that was once all but dead. They've saved the land for both our food supply and our ecological life support systems. They're at the core of one of the great economic transitions in human history.

So all we can say is….more power to the turbine tower "color wars"….and more wind power to us all!

Buffalo Biomass

As we lean back in our high-flying, sun-powered cabin, the plains stretch out beneath us like a mighty green ocean.

From our high-tech, west-moving perch we can make out, at the base of some turbine towers, a herd of mighty bison nudging the painted steel. Some have rubbed it shiny, scratching their scruffy backs in ancient pleasure.

The buffalo have elbowed the beef cattle out of Windiana. They roam wild and strong. They don't need the corn and soy once raised, amazingly enough, to lard up those clunky beefers for slaughter. In the days of heart disease and pesticides, critics charged that cholesterol, not food, was the primary product of American plains agriculture.

Not to mention growth hormones, chemical runoff and genetic mutations. Or the serial disasters of Mad Cow Disease, avian flu and a dozen other plagues, one right after the other, whose devastation defied belief and almost killed us all.

As the human and animal death toll soared and the birth rate plummeted from the eco-catastrophes of the Fossil/Nuke Apocalypse, debate raged over what those who survived were going to eat.

Much of it focussed on meat. As they have for centuries, millions of militant vegetarians argue that killing animals for food is just plain wrong. After the plagues of the early 21st Century, their ranks have vastly multiplied.

Today's new "Vegetopians" are loosely allied with the "Concerned Carnivores" who are ambivalent about animal rights as a moral issue, but who warn that factory farming ruins too much land, grain and water. Few industries, they say, have been more ecologically destructive or murderously plague-ridden than the corporate mass production of milk, beef, pork, chicken and eggs.

Before Solartopia, tens of millions of hapless animals were concentrated in tiny, manure-laden pens and deathly high-rises. In unspeakable conditions, most never saw the light of day. Many were indescribably altered.

These hellish beef, pork, chicken and dairy mills bred Biblical insect plagues that swarmed over the countryside. Millions of tons of manure washed into rivers, lakes and the oceans, inflicting horrific destruction, wiping out whole species of marine life.

Solartopia has ended all that.

We have no consensus on the moral question of eating animals. Nor do we expect one. The Vegetopians who deem it wrong are growing in number. The edge to their argument has been sharpened by the death toll from the disease-born plagues and eco-damage of yesterday's corporate meat industry.

But in today's global food fight, the "pro-life" vegans and "die-hard" meat eaters still light up the talk shows around dinner time.

The mighty buffalo are a prime topic. Like the fish that run wild in the sea, revived and thriving beneath those offshore co-gen complexes, the bison roam over huge stretches of terrain where once far costlier cattle ranged.

When hard times hit, the tough, evolved prairie bison proved sustainable. Commercial cattle, with their feed lots and grain dependencies, did not.

Today's buffalo are a beneficial "companion crop" for the wind and bio-fuel industries. Except for the occasional back scratch, they are no bother to the turbines, whose footprint on the land is minimal.

They graze in harmony with the amber waves of energy crops that profitably cover so much of Windiana. They pay back what they eat in soil-enriching bison chips, spread as they have been for thousands of years.

May they continue to do so for thousands more.

Grow Your Own Organic Building

Carefully regulated by number and health, Solartopia's beloved buffalo feed on and amidst the same switchgrass and hemp, Jerusalem artichoke and poplar trees, that help power subways in Manhattan and light skyscrapers in Seattle.

These sturdy perennials grow fast, on their own, every year, without chemical fertilizers or the plough, without pesticides or herbicides.

Hemp gives the world its paper supply and its best clothing fiber. The oil from its seeds is highly prized for too many really far out uses to keep straight. Our most universally loved of all cash crops, industrial cannabis is so hugely profitable and so spiritually essential that the family farmers it saved still can't believe it was once illegal.

With increasingly sophisticated organic methods, cross-plantings and computerized eco-management, the business of bio-fuels has soared into the trillions. It has thrived in part from an agricultural surprise: bio-building materials.

The 2001 terror attacks spread a lethal cloud of incinerated toxics all over New York City. A terrible health disaster ensued. The CONG corporations hid the real scope of the chemical carnage. But inorganic plastics, asbestos, fiberglass, concrete, window glass and other carcinogenic dust fed a devastating plague of airborne illness that still scars the soul of the city and the lungs of its people.

 The studies and the bitter controversy dragged on. But Solartopia knew it could not continue building with toxic substances and expect to live in good health. The green construction movement took on new urgency and gained new clout.

Against all odds, chlorinated plastics and a very wide range of toxic building materials have been phased out. Banned for decades, their lingering residues still plague us.

In their place has come an astounding array of organic substitutes.

In the early 1900s, Henry Ford wanted automobiles made entirely out of soy-based plastics and other farm-raised materials. He saw a future

transportation system built on (and powered by) living crops, not dead fossils. The vision was buried in cheap oil…at least for a century.

In Solartopia, that dream has redefined the structures in which we live.

Where endless fields of soy once went to fatten cattle and harden arteries, now they feed the bio-plastics that permeate every building, vehicle, and consumer product we use.

Hemp supplies an endless array of fabrics, paints, rope and structural materials, plus most of the world's paper. Bamboo does things in structures one could never dream of doing with steel and concrete. Natural substitutes have been found for toxic PVC, poisonous fiberglass and much more. Carbon and more exotic composites are finding their way into buildings and vehicles. Most of the iron and steel, copper and aluminum we use comes from sources which are re-used, recycled and re-used again. As the Apollo laws put it: nothing can be made here that can't be re-used.

The process is far from complete. Solartopia still forges plenty of "old style" iron and steel, copper and concrete.

Someday, in our brave renewable world, we look to a law requiring that EVERYTHING be built entirely of organic materials, grown with zero impact on our much-relieved Mother Earth.

We're not totally there yet, but soon …

The Eclectic Electric Desert

Our silent journey continues ever westward. Beneath us, at last, gleams the great PV heartland.

Nuke weapons were once tested here. Then King CONG tried to stuff the place with radioactive waste. The dormant volcano at Yucca Mountain was once drilled with a $10 billion tunnel-and-train gizmo meant to accept huge quantities of spent reactor rods. Now it's now just another off-beat tourist attraction, with slot machines in the caverns and a spa in one of the would-have-been waste chambers.

From the endless arid deserts that surround the place, huge photovoltaic arrays stare up at the sun. They send cheap, clean electricity pouring into El Paso, Las Vegas, Denver, Albuquerque, Phoenix, Los Angeles.

One massive solar square stands out. Long ago, Solartopian pioneers covered a thousand square miles of Shoshone land with primitive PV. With the tribe's blessing, the flat plates of this National Emergency Backup PV Array shine up at us like an ancient shimmering shrine.

This is the world's largest single PV power center. At the peak of the oil and terror wars, it was capable in an emergency (or otherwise) of producing the equivalent of the whole nation's electric supply. It was meant to both guarantee our national security…and to make a statement.

Today it still works. It reminds the world that when we had to, America kicked its addiction to eco-deadly energy.

It was expensive. But it was far far cheaper than the endless, futile petro-slaughters that raged through the early years of the new millennium.

Most of America's solar cells track the sun from urban rooftops. There are no transmission costs. Solartopia's buildings generally power themselves.

But here we see thousands of spin-off "PV plantations" stretching for miles in all desert directions.

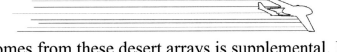

The electricity that comes from these desert arrays is supplemental. It's used, when needed, in mass transit, heavy industry, hospitals, and other infrastructure.

It's as good to have at hand as it is to see.

The Power Towers

Around and about those flat plate PV plantations, power towers thrust themselves into the air like giant desert candles. Some are a hundred feet high, some even more.

These phallic generators are regularly lampooned on evening talk shows as some kind of primitive sex symbol. They turn up everywhere in Solartopian literature, like a Greek revival gone green. One neo-pagan anthropologist has even written them a love poem. (He says it's a satire; I'm not convinced.)

Whatever their "larger meaning," these are the tallest structures in the desert. Their shafts stand erect above the gritty plain. Encased in their rounded tips are hot boilers. A heavy heat-exchanging liquid spurts its way through, exciting the turbines below while procreating significant juice.

Surrounding the towers at the base are massive arrays of mirrors (that nutty psycho-babbler calls them "vernal sun slaves") that gyrate from dawn to dusk in diurnal rhythms. En masse, they lavish their solar rays onto the tips of the towers with exquisite intensity. The focussed light is blinding. The intense heat boils the exchange medium and makes those turbines throb.

Nearly abandoned in the early 2000s, these power towers have a potent reputation for filling big investment openings in a highly satisfying manner.

A second type of power tower has recently joined the array. Pioneered in Australia, these are huge, hollow tubes built with openings at top and bottom. In the heat of the day, powerful "nooner" winds are sucked through the shafts, whose southern skins are lined with PV. The surging energy is captured and converted by turbines that spin inside.

The two breeds of Solartopian sun shafts have joined those decorated turbine towers as some of our most popular tourist sites. In this age of peace and prosperity, few things seem more exciting than taking the family out to the desert, and listening to desert winds howl through vertical tunnels sometimes five hundred feet high. Or donning sun glasses and meditating on the intense power of 1000-degree sunlight as focussed on a massive boiler perched a hundred feet in the air.

This has to be a major leap forward when you consider that eighty years ago, in the 1950s, thousands of Americans did much the same thing for intensely radioactive atomic bomb tests. To our knowledge, no one has yet died from the fallout of taking in a power tower's shiny tip.

These sprawling PV fields and towering solar candles pour their essence all over the urban/suburban southwest. The sun-driven electrons do for the grateful Electric Desert what prairie gusts do for Windiana. By all accounts, it's good for both of them.

Together they help provide the stable, baseload green muscle for a deeply satisfying prosperity that, over the long term, renders Solartopians of all persuasions positively ecstatic.

Dramatically, the electric desert gives way to the mountainous corridors that open into the southern California megalopolis.

Thousands of startling trough mirrors stretch out to the north of our flight path. These long, low, lithe concave arrays track the daily sun. They focus its rays on horizontal tubes filled with heat-exchanging liquids like the ones atop the power towers. The super-hot energy carriers then fire up boilers that turn turbines. They're backed by bio-fuels that burn through the night. When needed, these sleek, graceful co-generators can produce base-load green power all day, every day.

Trough array technology was pioneered and installed in the 1980s by an Israeli firm called Luz. The plants always worked well. But the financing was cynically sabotaged by California Governor George Deukmejian, a Reagan-Era Luddite.

Deukmejian did to Governor Jerry Brown's pioneer Solartopian programs what Ike and Reagan did nationwide. In the service of King CONG, Deukmejian drove the Golden State's nascent renewable energy business into tragic retreat. He torpedoed Luz and a countless other solar startups.

With them California lost its early chance to avoid energy chaos. Not to mention ten thousand jobs and the world's leadership in what eventually became a trillion-dollar industry.

The Luz technology barely survived. It took off in Spain. Then it revived here. Now it thrives with a thousand-fold the deployed capacity. Looking north, we see the original arrays surrounded by hordes of new, more powerful siblings, tracking the daily sun, pouring out the solar juice.

Up and down the Sierra ridges are the wind farms. To our south is Kumeyaay, California's first big native-sited turbine array. Since 2005 it has vastly enriched the Campo tribe on whose land it sits. Sited just north of the Mexican border, its original 50 megawatt phalanx of Gamesa (Spanish) turbines shows no signs of slowing down. Dozens more like it make the Sierra ridgeline look like a long, twirling Disney attraction.

A lot of locals once hated this wind farm. But when the bottom line turned from red to green, the welcome mat came out like magic. With their rainbow hues and seductive shimmy, these Solartopian stalwarts are as firmly embraced here as they are back east in the Windiana prairies.

The arid corridors at Palm Springs and Tehachapi still sport a few odd desert breeze geezers. Like those old rusty Volvos with a few million miles on them (they last longer on bio-fuels) these sturdy green elders have been left up for the hell of it. Las Vegas gives odds on how long they'll last. So far, there have been only losers.

Most 1980s originals have been raided for spare parts and melted in solar ovens. Their aging bodies have been recycled into reborn tubular towers and turbine internals that let them spin again.

For fifty years this powerful "desert wind tunnel" has hosted successive generations of ever-better machines. Like giant sunflowers whose petals ceaselessly twirl, these gentle giants grace the southern California megalopolis with green juice in quantities---and at prices---that were once the stuff of utopian fantasy.

The Enron Apocalypse

The renewable revolution that saved us all could have happened long before it did. The huge wind farms and power towers, solar arrays and offshore

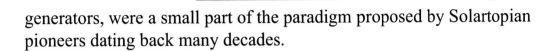

generators, were a small part of the paradigm proposed by Solartopian pioneers dating back many decades.

In the 1990s these prescient visionaries demanded California install some 600 megawatts of wind, solar and other natural power. They warned of a coming crisis. They predicted---correctly---that the state needed a green cushion to protect itself from CONG utilities and corporate power constrictors, many coiled up in Enron's "Texas Oiligarchy."

By today's standards, what the activists wanted was a tiny pittance, designed to give the public a modicum of energy security. But Southern California Edison and other predatory utilities were out to protect their investments in four absurdly expensive atomic reactors stuck on earthquake faults at San Onofre and Diablo Canyon.

So Solartopia was postponed. And we know all too well what happened to those nukes.

Meanwhile, Kenneth Lay's infamous Enron and its Texas cohorts robbed California of $100 billion. The Golden State's economy and ecology were devastated. Much of America soon followed them down.

The long nightmare of financial bankruptcy and radioactive panic, of poverty and despair, war and dictatorship, all could and should have been avoided. With just a pinch of Solartopian common sense, California's 2000-2001 deregulation fiasco and fossil/nuke nightmare need not have happened.

Amidst the economic and ecological carnage, a cry came out from the grassroots:

NEVER AGAIN!

The Murder of the Red Line

Flying into the airspace above the former Mecca of petro-smog and black lung, gridlock and reactor death, the fruits of our hard-fought Solartopian triumph become obvious.

The gargantuan highway system that paved over the land, blackened the air and destroyed the health of the Los Angeles basin slowly, gratefully turned green. H, PV and bio-fuels have revolutionized transportation.

Enron's was not the only CONG catastrophe to abuse our future. Next to the murder of the Red Line, it was déjà vu all over again.

A century ago, as the first incarnation of America's magnificent mass transit system achieved its peak, Los Angeles was revered worldwide for a trolley network unique in its range and efficiency.

Angelinos loved their Red Line. Her many tributaries stretched from the Santa Monica shore deep into the valleys and deserts. With the Red Line at its heart, the southern California trolley system throbbed with thousands of riders and the essential life force of a booming young metropolis.

Then it was murdered.

We Solartopians view the infamous slaughter of America's passenger rail/mass transit system as the eco-crime of the 20th Century.

In the 1950s, the corporate automobile, oil, glass and rubber magnates were put on trial in downtown L.A. But the history of that case was hidden for decades.

Hollywood briefly touched on the disaster in the quirky cartoon hybrid *Who Framed Roger Rabbit?*, a loud, wacky comedy about leveling "Toon Town" to build the first freeway cloverleaf.

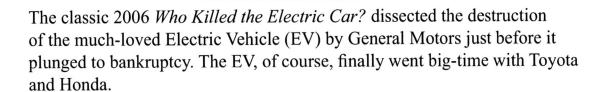

The classic 2006 *Who Killed the Electric Car?* dissected the destruction of the much-loved Electric Vehicle (EV) by General Motors just before it plunged to bankruptcy. The EV, of course, finally went big-time with Toyota and Honda.

Then came the iconic documentary *Murder of the Red Line.* Viewers still weep to see King CONG pitching those beautiful trolley cars in the trash or oceans, to rot and rust. They yell in outrage as Detroit's are sold to the city of Hiroshima. They howl in anger as others just seem to vanish in the corporate air.

Destroying those quaint little "tin cans on rails" cost us billions to replace and trillions in needless carbon emissions. By century's end, our million miles of highway concrete were hopelessly strangled. L.A. choked on the gas-fired automobile and its noisy, global-warmed, anti-human ugliness.

Viewers howl as passenger rail service disappears. They cheer as a California jury convicts General Motors and its cohorts of mass industrial murder.

But when a token ($5,000) slap is all the court system can muster, in a ritual now familiar to millions, angry Solartopian viewers rise up vowing to do something about it.

And so they have.

A Revolution Never Again to be Denied

From our clean, green H-airliner we can see the thin silver rails of the reborn Red Line. Our hybridized mass transit system thrives on computerized mag-lev trains and hand-driven toon-town trolleys, bio-fueled H-highways and body-powered bikes, ultra-efficient people movers and beautifully restored organic landscapes.

The lethal connections between the murder of American mass transit, the 2001 terror attacks and global warming's terrible toll are memorialized at the National Museum of Mass Transit in downtown LA. Its centerpiece is a scale model of the restored southern California system, centered on the Red Line. Packed with retro trains and relic trolleys, classic electric cars and speedy high-tech bikes, it teaches a new generation of Solartopians what it really means to get around.

The museum is linked to monuments at the World Trade Center and New Orleans's Congo Square, where every Sunday we scorn in blues the criminal incompetence that temporarily wrecked that brave city.

All three sites are solar-powered. They herald our Brave Renewable World.

They also enshrine the Solartopian belief that the eco-catastrophes of the 20th Century need not have occurred.

As befits a society that loves to argue, the debate among the scholars and historians still fiercely rages. But most Solartopians now accept as fact the idea that the green revolution was repeatedly sabotaged by King CONG and its corporate co-conspirators.

They argue that the murder of the Red Line was only the most obvious and egregious of the eco-crimes of the 20th Century.

And they highlight the Solartopian pride that those who perpetrated the "eco-crimes of the century" were made to pay in special ways.

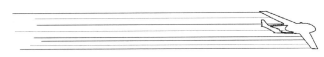

After Enron, Californians knew what had to be done. Putting the perpetrators behind bars was highly satisfying. But insufficient.

To guarantee our survival, Solartopians began ripping apart the corporate barriers against renewables---and then the corporations themselves.

As in Windiana, the heart of this Solartopian revolution has been public power. California's early standard bearer was the Sacramento Municipal Utility District (SMUD), proud champion of municipal ownership.

The demand of the public to own and operate its own electric utilities came at the creation. As Thomas Edison and Charles Brush introduced New York and Cleveland to the realities of electric power in the 1880s, city dwellers demanded direct control.

The warfare between private and public utilities was instant. Municipal-owned utilities ("munis") put their customers before profits. The Investor Owned Utilities (IOUs) saw it the other way around.

For more than a century, the munis delivered cheaper, more reliable electricity. But the IOUs rode the tides of corporate greed and government corruption. Until the dawn of Solartopia, they monopolized 80% of America's electric power.

The munis did make their share of mistakes. Some built trash-burning power plants, which proved to be both horrendous polluters and financial disasters. Others, like SMUD, even built nuke reactors.

But after then-Mayor Kucinich saved its Muni Light system, Cleveland became America's first North Coast city to install a wind turbine in its downtown.

And as King CONG cracked, those lucky communities that owned their own utilities became the envy---and role model---for the Solartopian Revolution.

On June 5, 1989, SMUD broke new ground. Its owner-ratepayers voted to shut the failed Rancho Seco reactor, and to plunge into renewables. Solartopia now celebrates the moment with a national holiday.

At the head of every SMUD-Day parade is that poster child for green power, the famed photograph showing Sacramento's dead Rancho Seco nuke flanked by solar cells. A half-century after they were instilled, the PV still pumps out the juice!

Community ownership made it all happen. When Sacramento citizens voted to shut Rancho Seco, it actually went cold the next day. Imagine that!

SMUD then invested in wind and solar. It planted thousands of shade trees to slash air conditioning demand. It gave rebates for trade-ins on inefficient refrigerators.

And when Enron gouged the state for $100 billion in that phony energy crisis, Sacramento proved immune. Throughout California, cities, towns and counties took control of their own power supplies.

Davis and other surrounding towns joined SMUD. San Francisco lost a major public power vote when Pacific Gas & Electric pitched key ballot boxes into the Bay. But by a 3:1 margin, it approved a $100 million solar bond. Then the city installed a 4-megawatt array atop the downtown Moscone Center.

PV now covers all San Francisco's south-facing walls, and all rooftops not planted in gardens. Dozens of California cities soon passed similar solar bonds. Wind, PV, efficiency, green rooftops, mass transit---they all sprouted like hemp in the Mendocino spring.

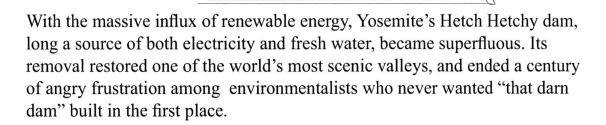

With the massive influx of renewable energy, Yosemite's Hetch Hetchy dam, long a source of both electricity and fresh water, became superfluous. Its removal restored one of the world's most scenic valleys, and ended a century of angry frustration among environmentalists who never wanted "that darn dam" built in the first place.

Long-lost riverine eco-systems have been reborn. Fish now swim where waters had ceased to flow. Scores of endangered species are back from the brink of extinction.

So is American democracy.

With SMUD as our poster child, Solartopian communities of all shapes and sizes have grabbed their power systems for green public ownership.

In Hull, Massachusetts… Long Island, New York… Bowling Green… Cleveland… Nebraska Public Power… Colorado Springs…one after the other, a tsunami of public-owned entities jumped into renewables. School districts and individual businesses cut loose from their utility companies and built their own renewable generators.

Freed from corporate domination, the global economy now marches to the tune of democratic decentralization. In the Solartopian business of selling electricity, the IOU has gone the way of the nuclear power plant and the internal combustion automobile.

The Four Green Horses of the Anti-Apocalypse

So has the clout of King CONG. Early No Nukers said taking money from fossil/nukes and using it for solar and efficiency would create millions of jobs. If it was good for the environment, it would be good for the economy.

This article of faith was sorely tested. Some green technologies fizzled. Many locations didn't work. Critical projects crashed from poor planning. A few were killed by public opposition.

But next to the eco-financial catastrophes of burning fossil fuels and suffering nuclear power plants, Solartopia's failures barely constitute chump change.

Economically, nukes were buried three times: first by error, then by terror, and all along the way by the falling costs of wind, PV and bio-fuels. Periodic attempts to revive this most un-competitive of all industries still draw painful laughs on late-night TV.

For when cooler heads looked at the real numbers, they saw what should have been obvious since the 1952 publication of the Paley Report: financially, atomic reactors could never cut it. Only huge government subsidies and insurance protection kept them going. And all that finally did stop.

Ditto fossil fuels, with their unsustainable ancillary costs. Eventually, simple economics made it clear that the world had no choice but to go solar. Green became the color of both money and survival.

Sensing sustainable profits and a social future, Goldman Sachs, John Deere, Warren Buffett, General Electric, Edison Capital and their cohorts triggered the Great Green Gold Rush, that glorious avalanche of renewable cash that has never stopped pouring into Solartopian investments.

Community ownership, social justice, sustainable prosperity and ecological harmony became the Four Green Horses of the anti-Apocalypse. They carried the Solartopian impulse from a fringe movement to the new dominant paradigm.

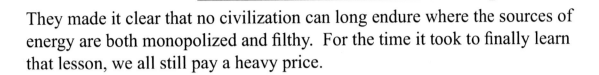

They made it clear that no civilization can long endure where the sources of energy are both monopolized and filthy. For the time it took to finally learn that lesson, we all still pay a heavy price.

Nor do we have an end to disease and famine. Crime, violence, injustice, stupidity, the impulse to war---they are all still with us. People are still people.

But the great green deluge has brought us a holistic new way of doing business.

Solarizing the Corporation

Where the clan, tribe, city-state, empire, church, monarch and nation-state once organized human economies, in the Industrial Revolution it was the corporation. With globalization, it became the multi-national.

These were the vehicles that accumulated the cash and organizational clout that powered our progress. In their later stages, the multi-nationals tied together the globe. In some cases they built the networks and researched, financed and developed the technical and administrative breakthroughs that made Solartopia possible .

But as they broke free of geographic, financial and legal restraints, they came to dominate the public that licensed them. Though their PR often said otherwise, profit became their only motive. They became far too big and powerful to be bothered with the details of human and ecological accountability. With globalization, the mega-corporations---led by King CONG---grabbed unsustainable levels of range and power.

And like so many mega-organizations before them, they over-reached. Or, as our historians put it, they "Enronized," a term now defined in our *Encyclopedia* as "the process by which large corporations spontaneously disintegrate in toxic clouds of dishonesty, dishonor, theft and greed."

There have certainly been notable exceptions. Some things in Solartopia require organizational structures with a truly global reach.

But overall, at the Solartopian dawn, the bulk of our centralized, hierarchical corporations became dinosaurs---unwieldy, inefficient, un-manageable, anti-democratic, obsolete. Those that could not make the transition to public and ecological accountability---whose extreme concentrations of wealth and power became unsustainable in organizational, human and ecological terms---these went, simply, extinct.

Amidst climate chaos and wars for oil, under irresistible social and financial pressures, globalization was brought to heel.

Key to the transformation was a new accounting for human and ecological costs. Carbon taxes and value assessments for the tangible impacts of radioactive waste, polluted streams, global warming and industrial assaults on public health radically shifted the financial matrix.

When confronted with an accurate pricing system for the true negatives of their polluting businesses, King CONG and its corporate minions were forced to redefine themselves.

When they couldn't or wouldn't, the public did it for them. When necessary, in our hyper-linked age of eco-accountability, states, cities, towns, counties, tribes, cooperatives, communities, unions, individual businesses, homeowners, families and activists simply tore the big conglomerates and the terrain they dominated into manageable, human-scale units.

It wasn't clean or easy. It didn't happen overnight. But it had to be done.

Today our messy, ever-evolving economic mosaic rides the efficiencies of the competitive market and entrepreneurial drive. But it serves the core needs of humankind as a whole and the ecological demands of this wonderful---but exacting---organism we call Earth.

It is the worst system the world has ever seen---except for all the other ones.

Above all, the institutions that organize our economy serve rather than rule.

Gargantuan CEO salaries are gone. The Solartopian rich are less richer than the rest of us. The no-longer-so-poor have options, and a floor on which to stand. We all have our dignity.

Nobody starves in Solartopia. All are educated for free, the key to a healthy populace capable of competing and prospering in a hyper-technical age. (Long ago, all education-related debts, including residual student loans, were wiped clean).

Our sustainable small farms have been re-established. Our food is cleanly grown and abundant. Our schools generate their own power, grow their own lunch and thrive on the money that used to fund a military that now fights no more wars for oil.

Health care, transportation, solarized housing, clean air and water are no longer the sole province of the specially privileged.

Our big cities, now so very rich, are squeaky clean. Reborn mass transit has cured our petro-addiction. Grid-lock is gone from our transportation system, our rivers, our souls.

In short: Greening has overtaken and redefined globalization. King CONG's precocious offspring have been tamed and trained, downsized and domesticated….and put to beautiful use.

Mother Knows Best

All this has come in synch with the Feminine Ascent.

At the Solartopian dawn, women were a majority of the American electorate, and of the students in US universities and law schools. In 2006, a female became the first Speaker of the US House. As of 2030, three have served as Chief Executive, including the Latina (our first) who is now in her second term.

One of our spiritual anthropologists calls this "a cosmic union, at last, between the invading European techno-patriarchs and the earthy matriarchs of native America." She says our "ancient indigenous better half is asserting herself through a cultural economy being re-rooted in community and nature."

As you might guess, this analysis doesn't fly very far in some of our rowdier sports bars.

But there's clearly been an impact on population growth. From the Malthusian dawn of the Industrial Revolution, the warnings have blared about "too many people" sinking the planet.

Our diverse, feisty Solartopian society has reached no firm religious, intellectual or ideological consensus on birth control, abortion, gay marriage, artificial insemination, cloning…none of that.

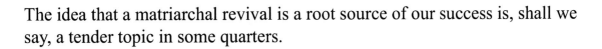

The idea that a matriarchal revival is a root source of our success is, shall we say, a tender topic in some quarters.

But only a handful of countries have not yet elected a female leader. And since the Era of Saint Oprah, there are no issues of sexuality and reproduction that we won't loudly debate. (It is virtually impossible to embarrass a Solartopian.)

Radioactive emissions, global warming, famine, disease and war have all had their hand in dimming the human birth rate. And (thankfully!) the battle of the sexes rages as ever.

But wherever prosperity and universal education mate with equal rights among the genders, the birth rate seems inclined to harmonize with how many of us Mother Earth wants to accommodate.

Solartopia Reclaims Altamont

Humans are still what they are. Solartopia is not paradise. And, at birth, it still had wind wounds to heal.

In the pioneer 1980s, primitive turbine arrays were installed at Altamont Pass, in the mountain reaches east of San Francisco. Many were good, solid units. But others were badly made. They were sited primarily for state tax credits. They performed poorly. And they killed birds.

Most were mounted on lattice-work towers. Unfortunately, in the unique canyon that is Altamont, endangered raptors perched on the cross-bars. When they spotted their ground squirrel dinner, they dove through the spinning blades. Too many got clunked.

Over time, hundreds of raptors died. It was a PR bonanza for King CONG's bilious bloviators. Without a hint of irony, the most lethal industry in eco-history complained that renewable energy was bad for birds.

Funded mightily by the fossil/nuke cartels, the right wing "think tanks" launched an anti-wind blitzkrieg. They blithely extrapolated the avian kill calculations at Altamont and solemnly warned that windmills would soon destroy every bird on Earth. They claimed that only reactor radiation and global warming could guarantee an avian future.

There have been other well-publicized surprises for the wind industry, such as occasional bat kills and charges of stroboscopic health effects. But as of today, the Exxon Valdez has killed more birds and other animals in one day than have all the world's windmills for half a century.

All across Windiana, out at sea, along the ridge-tops and wherever else modern turbines have been sited, the bird kill has been virtually nil… dwarfed by the pre-Solartopian slaughter of billions by moving automobiles, guy-wired cell towers, glass-paned skyscrapers, house cats gone wild and the horrifying plagues of avian flu, West Nile Virus and so many other diseases born of global warming and pollution. All that, we stopped.

Hammered by a grassroots campaign, Altamont's owners replaced the lattice towers with tubular jobs that are cheaper to maintain (and more fun to decorate). Raptors cannot perch on them. The arrays are bigger, slower and far more profitable. The death toll has plummeted. So has the bum PR.

The irony of environmentalists fighting each other over an already-installed wind farm was a sure sign Solartopia had come of age.

Lessons were learned at Altamont. Since the Solartopian dawn, every turbine siting has been studied, re-studied and then studied again. Today, the death of a bird at a wind farm is as rare as the latest laughable threat of an OPEC oil embargo. We're heading somewhere!

PETE SEEGER'S "SONG FOR SOLARTOPIA!"

In early 2007, the legendary folksinger Pete Seeger penned the classic anthem *Song for Solartopia*. In the spirit of the Green Revolution, he put out a call for verses, and offered this sage advice:

"An editorial is not a song. Tell a story, paint a picture, make people smile."

Since then, tens of thousands of Solartopians have sent their words to **www.solartopia.org**, where Pete's original chorus can still be heard.

> *Verses need to paint a picture, tell a story: A gang of young people getting jobs and saving the world*
>
> *Pete*

Over the years, collections of the verses have been posted and spread throughout Solartopia. You are more than welcome to contribute your own.

WONDERFUL

SOLARTOPIAN

LOS ANGELES!

As our silent H-airliner heads into the late afternoon, we sail over the shrine at Thousand Palms, where the brave renewable world of sun-powered mass transit dawned early.

In 1998---even before that first public commercial H station opened in Hamburg---the Sunline Transit System began pumping H into the southern California bus system.

Unlike Hamburg, the hydrogen that still feeds the big bus and trolley system for Thousand Palms comes from solar juice. Rooftop PV zaps the water and moves the H right into the fuel cells. The pure oxygen is still sold on the open market. An LED array tells us all how much juice this thing has generated.

As we fly over the desert vastness that is Los Angeles, ten thousand such H-stations pump out clean power.

It's one of history's great ironies that L.A. became America's ultimate Solartopian showcase. In the very big business that is now southwestern solar power, the PV mega-farms burn bright throughout the L.A. canyons. Desert candles do their thing. Trough mirrors curl and shine in the sun. In the ridges and arroyos, turbines spin green gold. Photovoltaics cover every rooftop that isn't planted in a desert garden.

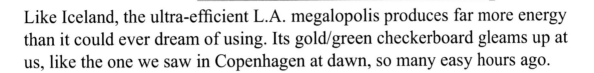

Like Iceland, the ultra-efficient L.A. megalopolis produces far more energy than it could ever dream of using. Its gold/green checkerboard gleams up at us, like the one we saw in Copenhagen at dawn, so many easy hours ago.

On the garden rooftops, in the parks and backyards, along what used to be the freeway system and in the heart of downtown, food is grown. The bird-filled greenery cools and cleans the urban air. The eco-heart of the reborn megalopolis beats to the healthy pulse of an urban mega-garden… and "green lungs" that work. Cactus and aloe, palmettos and almonds, pomegranate and pineapple… they thrive in harmony amidst and above L.A. 'hoods that once seethed in anger from poverty and pollution.

Today, L.A. chills in the soothing, cooling green of Solartopian prosperity. The photovoltaic cells that rise and shine from southern California's rooftops light and cool the buildings on which they sit, along with the vehicles that move between them.

There are no transmission costs. Most southern Californians get all their energy from the homes and condos in which they live. Some jump out their front doors into public and private vehicles that are hyper-charged with excess H and electricity that trickled overnight from basement batteries and fuel cells, charged by yesterday's sun.

Just a few decades ago, this city was hooked as if on drugs. Massive power-lines mainlined juice from the King CONG pushers---fossil burners and nuke reactors---that nearly killed us all.

The H-stations have helped to revamp and revive the city's magnificent re-born Red Line transit system. Backup power pours in from the Palm Springs wind mills and Mojave Luz generators, the Needles power towers and Shoshone solar farms. L.A.'s infamously filthy air has turned blue and clean.

Sleek commuter trains traverse a hybridized freeway system that resembles the original in name only. Valley ridge lines sport gaudily painted mega-turbines, their towers often hyping the latest films.

Stylish designer compost heaps thrive in a million cinematic gardens. A million more methane digesters transform kitchen and human wastes to Solartopian bio-fuel.

As in Iceland, deep geothermal wells capture the Earth's inner fires, and make the megalopolis even more solidly self-sufficient. All up and down the west coast, this primeval power source adds to the cushion that has rendered Solartopia rich.

But in our hyper-efficient age, consumption levels are actually lower than they were in the 1990s. From superconducting to mag-lev, from LED lighting to ten million tight, bright, self-sufficient homes and offices…waste and pollution have been banished and banned.

Everywhere we look, Los Angelinos have shined up the desert, cleansed the parks and rivers, purified the surf and shoreline.

The unspeakable sewage that befouled the coast is an unmentioned memory. The glistening beaches and brilliant blue waters of the Santa Monica Basin are pristine and swimmable. They abound with fish and surfers, snorkelers and scuba divers. Schoolchildren gather in fascination around teeming tide pools.

It could have happened quicker. There should have been fewer casualties, human and ecological.

But against all odds, L.A. has become a great green icon. It has kicked back for a Solartopian party meant to last, dude.

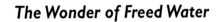

The Wonder of Freed Water

Out to sea, we see another epic range of gigantic ocean co-generators, like the ones in the Baltic and Atlantic. These pump pure green H and electricity back to L.A., along with some of its freshest, cleanest water. The huge aquaducts that drained the high Sierras have long since become the world's longest recreational waterslide.

Back to the north, the Hetch-Hetchy dam has come down. So have the Glen Canyon, the Boulder and many more throughout North America. In Egypt, the Aswan. In China, the massive Three Gorges dam----finished less than three decades ago---has been totally removed.

The unlikely demise of these huge hydro projects has been one of the great surprises of the Solartopian age.

But, as the millennium progressed, the ultimate issue defining the future of humankind was neither oil nor power. It was water. Wherever we looked, global warming fried forestland into desert. Lakes like California's Mono and Russia's Baikal and Africa's Victoria dried up and disappeared. The rivers that had defined civilization itself---the Tigris, Euphrates, Nile, Danube, Yellow, Yangtze, Colorado, Columbia, and so many more, no longer even reached the sea.

It was mostly about climate chaos. But the industrial abuse of water, the massive mis-use of irrigation, the careless waste of our most precious resource, the source of all life, could not be blamed on a single failing. All we knew for sure was that something was desperately out of balance. Without restoring our aquatic eco-systems, we would perish.

As Solartopian technology poured green energy into the global grid, the power from these monster hydro facilities became moot. Eco-scientists showed again and again that the billions of tons of concrete killing the free-flow of our natural waters were toxic in too many ways to tolerate.

So, one by one, amidst bitter controversy and incredulity, followed by ecstatic release and indescribable joy, these monster dams came tumbling down. Free-floating river bobbers recaptured some of the energy. But riverine arteries opened for the first time in decades. The clear waters flowed out from captivity.

That wasn't all it took. But it was a beginning. Fresh waters again flowed to the sea. Fish swam home. The land began to revive. Trees cooled the Earth's surface. The rains returned. A blockage opened. The planet sighed.

We Chose Life

Heading ever toward the setting sun, our hybrid H-airliner provides us the supreme privilege of flying above a pristine Pacific that was once at the brink of death.

Stretching down from Alaska to Chile, countless mighty co-gen complexes form our staunchest line of defense against the return of the petro-beasts.

Far to our north, Prince William Sound still bleeds from the Exxon Valdez. The executives who caused the spill spent their end times in penance for oily seas and dying birds.

The Alaska pipelines that became perpetual targets for petro-terrorists are long since abandoned. Diablo Canyon and San Onofre, those two big California nukes built on earthquake faults, are seething monuments to the awful idiocy of the ultimate radioactive horror show.

Who today can comprehend gouging coal or pumping petro-fuels or spewing radiation all over a planet whose sun and winds, tides and bio-fuels so easily provide all the energy a sane civilization could ever need?

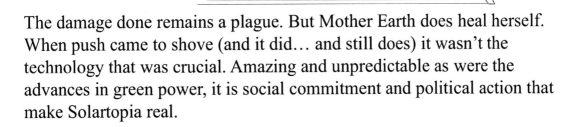

The damage done remains a plague. But Mother Earth does heal herself. When push came to shove (and it did… and still does) it wasn't the technology that was crucial. Amazing and unpredictable as were the advances in green power, it is social commitment and political action that make Solartopia real.

King CONG and its corporate minions seemed to have it all: the presidency, the Congress, the courts, the media, the money. But in the long run, fossil fuels and nuclear power were guns to our head. They threatened our rights and our freedoms, our jobs and our children, our economy and our survival. The damage was devastating, and ever escalating.

So the people had to fight. We used non-violent tactics never dreamed of, media we invented, levers of power we pulled out of nowhere, strategies that should never have worked. We suffered terrible, bloody, depressing defeats.

Our Solartopian liberation had been denied again and again. The hundred-year plague of the gas-fired automobile. The corrupt campaign against public power. The mid-century murder of our magnificent mass transit system. The 1950s denial of Harry Truman's pro-solar Paley Report. Ike's catastrophic 1953 wrong turn to nuclear power. The 1980s Reagan-Deukmejian anti-green rampage. Southern California Edison's veto of the 1990s green power initiative. Enron's turn-of-the-century hundred-billion-dollar price gouge. GM's burial of the EV. And through it all, the horrific, insanely expensive wars for oil for which we all still pay so dear.

But just when things seemed darkest, amidst the chaos and the rage, at the dawn of the Solartopian Age, the political, economic and spiritual dams somehow came down. With their riverine counterparts, the rushing waters of an epic change, too-long denied, finally burst through.

The heroic salmon are back in force. The Florida alligator, the Canada goose, and countless other near-extinct species have revived and thrived Most of all…US!

A million polluted sore spots are being reclaimed. Most coal mines have been filled, the mountain tops restored… as best we can. None will ever really be the same. Some sites are just dead dead dead. Some petro-nuke disease will never be fully eradicated. Some species will never return.

But as the whales spout and the dolphins dance in the mighty Pacific below, we remember that, when it really had to happen, we stopped those terminal, desperate wars for oil. We evicted and imprisoned those who started them. We ended the global terror they funded. We reversed their *putsch* toward dictatorship. We took back our democracy.

And all we did was finally deploy the renewable sources that had steadily evolved despite everything King CONG threw at them. The obstacles and the barriers, the stolen resources and buried patents, the lies and the detours…through it all, green power proved to be a force of nature, an unstoppable inevitability.

The tools for winning a totally sustainable planet were more than evident at the turn of the century, when the term *Solartopia* began to spread. In their basic forms, all the technology on which our brave renewable world is based today, in 2030, was available three decades ago.

Simply put: PV and its hyper-efficient green siblings did for energy in the first quarter of the 21st Century what the PC and internet did for the world of information in the last quarter of the 20th.

In our darkest hours, green power and defiant, irreverant non-violence fused with fiscal necessity and the eternal demands for social justice and biological survival to forge an economic and ecological revolution.

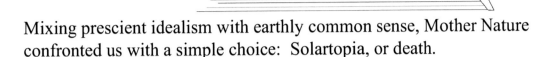

Mixing prescient idealism with earthly common sense, Mother Nature confronted us with a simple choice: Solartopia, or death.

WE CHOSE LIFE!

A Solartopian Aloha

Nowhere are the joys of that choice more abundant than in the Aloha State. With silent gratitude we fly gracefully into her setting sun.

Another magnificent line of giant co-generators stretches out to the horizon. In the dimming of the day, as we drop down toward Pearl Harbor, we can still see the outlines of tourist subs. Here and there, "schools" of snorkelers and scuba divers embrace the view.

In clear sight arise some of the earliest ocean thermal units. They are massive but simple, exploiting the tension between warm water at the surface and the colder ranges below.

These eco-powerhouses are anchored to Hawaii's steep volcanic ledges. Their huge tubes carry salty brine back and forth from solar-heated surface and the super-cool depths. Many are quietly married to nearby co-gen platforms that also harvest energy from the tides. Brightly painted wave worms ring the islands, carefully sited so as not to disrupt the *da kine* surfing spots.

As late as 2007, only the Aloha State was still dependent on electricity from oil. But as Solartopia rose, US Senator Spark Matsunaga rode its curl. His H-powered vision helped Hawaii pierce the final barriers to total energy self-sufficiency.

Industrial hemp for fuel and export joins once-illegal marijuana as the state's top cash crop. Geothermal energy from the ancient volcanoes that created this archipelago is harvested with all due reverence to Mesdammes Pele and Liluokalani, and those who honor them.

The sun, the ocean, the earth's core… Hawaii… like the rest of our gorgeous, giving planet… is blessed with all the green energy she could ever need.

As the state's motto puts it:

> *"Ua mau ke ia o ka'aina i ka pono…*
>
> *… the life of the land is preserved in righteousness".*

Mother Nature's Sun

In the twilight of today's Solartopian odyssey, we see the rainbow hues of a Pacific sun plunging with vibrant glory into the Far East.

We have flown from Europe to Hawaii without refueling. We touch down near a naval station once bombed by a nation desperate for fossil fuel. We are helped to land by tropical breezes that have made wars for oil a dimming, incomprehensible memory.

Solartopia has defused global terrorism, religious and otherwise. It de-funded the oil sheikdoms. It broke the petro-cartels. It shut the nukes that assaulted the earth while providing the ultimate targets for Apocalyptic terror.

Green energy saved our political rights (and vice-versa) and paved the way for social justice. Humanity has rushed into the vacuum left by King CONG and filled it with a work in progress full of hope and prosperity.

With a technological revolution barely imagined just twenty-five years ago, Solartopia has created a whole new level of global justice and prosperity. For our children and theirs, ecological survival is assured. Reasonable material comfort is a given. Where energy is cheap, clean, renewable and controlled by the public, all things are possible.

The global green machine we have created works silently, unobtrusively and with astonishing efficiency. It is sleek, clean and profitable. Above all, it sustains an infrastructure on which we can---must---live in both shared prosperity and calm harmony with the Earth that gave us birth.

Not least in this revolution, humankind is near a new level of natural awareness. In the 20th Century, the last of that tortured millennium, the Industrial Revolution became an angel of death.

In the polluted human soul, farm and field, sea and forest became less than natural, more like commodities. The sound of birds, the feel of woodlands, the joy of surf... they disappeared from our days.

We were alienated from our Mother Earth, even at war with her. The material wealth we gored and gouged proved to be dross and poison---and spiritually deadening.

It hasn't happened overnight. But the realities of our ancestral home seep back into our souls.

Unsustainable housing is coming down. Shoddy suburbs have decayed and collapsed. The land they temporarily subdued now takes them back, regains its fertility. The water tables they drained have refilled and overflow. Grass pokes through concrete. Streams rush over fallen dams. Newly planted trees cool and cleanse urban air. Falcons perch on skyscrapers. Owls fill urban parks. Big Sugar is out of the Everglades, which belongs again to the gators and sawgrass. Tobacco has shrunk to a specialty crop. Fruit and nut orchards line unsprayed golf courses that flourish with natural rainfall and a plethora of wildlife (they all seem to feature a little arboretum called "Tiger Woods").

Rail-based mass transit replaces and transcends a million square miles of obsolete highways and worthless concrete streets. Along alchemized transit lines, gorgeous forests of native species, from fruits to nuts, pines to palmettos, have poured back into our cities, our countryside, our souls.

Where once we traveled miles to visit the occasional surviving forests, as if they were aging oddities held in reserve, now our days are filled with birds and bees, seas and trees.

A quarter-century ago, skeptics might have taken a descriptive journal such as this to be a flight of pure fantasy, even whimsy. The idea that hyper-efficiency and sustainable energy could so thoroughly reshape our economy and our lives might have seemed to ancient readers to be purely wishful thinking. An impossible dream... lovely, but too unrealistic to be taken seriously.

What they'd miss is not only the regenerative power of these renewable technologies, but also---conversely---the killing power of the fossil/nuke apocalypse, and the choices it has forced.

Despite all we've accomplished, the jury is still out on whether we will survive global warming. Our ice caps have melted. A thousand coastal communities are under water. The weather patterns are disrupted and unpredictable. Diseases spread and species lost continue to threaten our existence and sadden our hearts. Petro-pollution and reactor emissions still plague our hearth and home.

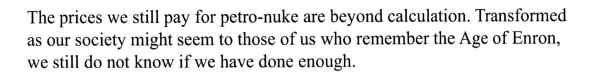

The prices we still pay for petro-nuke are beyond calculation. Transformed as our society might seem to those of us who remember the Age of Enron, we still do not know if we have done enough.

Every day, we wake up trying to figure out how to do more. Every night, we wonder where another hidden time bomb from King CONG's rotting residues will poison the progress we have made.

Yes, by honoring Mother Earth's irresistible demands, we have re-discovered her most precious gifts. Against all odds, we have acknowledged and overcome most of the radioactive, chemical and sprawled out pollutants of King CONG's war on human survival.

Today, our greatest hope is that this beautiful new generation of Solartopian children may find ways to live in ever-enhanced natural harmony. Theirs is now a recovering species that has barely survived, but knows it can thrive.

Far as we may have come, decades more of their full attention (and imagination) will be needed to guarantee their ultimate staying power. Their very lives depend on that hard-fought magical balance between material well-being, individual freedom, social justice and natural harmony.

Aloha... Sayonara... Namaste

In Hawaii, the dream was never quite lost. In the 1890s, this archipelago's queen, the great Liliuokalani, fought to save her nation's independence. She lost (temporarily) to the doleful barons of sugar and pineapple.

Her people remember.

Honolulu has become Solartopia's most diverse city. Her timeless roots in Mother Earth permeate the archipelago.

Tiny islands amidst a mammoth sea have little leeway for error.

The seeds of a new world, a Solartopian *Aloha*, project a powerful magnetism, and can help revive an entire planet.

We relax in our bio-hybrid taxi. We pass through a deep tropical forest of gorgeous palms and screeching parrots. The monorail above and trolleys around us wend their way through a mystic Valhalla, both urban and primeval, tropical and sweet. The only real terror we face here is from mischievous monkeys and falling coconuts.

How Honolulu transcended its traffic noise and awful over-crowding fills endless tracts on what we now revere as the *Solartopian miracle*.

Not an ounce of fossil fuel has been burnt here for years. Solartopian songs written today about the reconnection between humankind and nature, between the post-pollution world and the joys of a revived and modernized natural harmony, often start with the Aloha Isles, and the picturesque prosperity they've inspired worldwide.

But that's for another day, another H-airliner, another journal.

It's been a long, lovely journey. We arrive, gratefully, in our solar-cooled hotel. The sound of island birds and rustling leaves will soothe us to sleep. Tomorrow will be another day of clean, quiet travel through our Golden Green Age. Our Solartopian voyage will take us to Japan, China and India.

That's where our eco-revolution *really* tipped the global balance.

To be continued...

HELP US MOVE THE SOLARTOPIAN CLOCK!

The Solartopian Clock times and inspires our progress toward a totally green-powered planet.

Each number on the Clock stands for a year. The outer dial moves clockwise as we approach Solartopia.

We decide to move the dial based on the number and size of renewable installations made each year, the advancements of efficiency and conservation, and the rate at which fossil and nuclear power, and unsustainable waste, are being phased out.

Your comments, opinions, visualizations and hard information are part of the process.

The Solartopia.org web site is a rallying point. It includes a forum, chat room, blog and resource listings in both the renewables industry and among clean energy activist organizations. Our commitment is not merely to observe and evaluate the progress toward Solartopia, but to help make it happen.

We will see you at www.solartopia.org---and in Solartopia!

Thanks To

Polly Silverman; Dona & Bob Litowitz; Tom & Nancy Regan; Jerry Mander, Alvin Duskin & Randy Hayes, and the International Forum on Globalization; Michael Mariotte, the Nuclear Information & Resources Service & all who support it; Deb & the Nukebusters; Dan, Nina & the Keller family; Dan, Mary, Tyler & Corey Juhl; George, Leah & Tyler Crocker; Diane Rother; Ken Pentel; Paul & Sheila Wellstone & the good folks at the Wellstone Foundation; C-BED and the movement for farmer/community-owned renwables; Joe, John and the Ohio Farmers Union; David & Sarah Weiss and family; Bonnie Raitt & Kathy Kane; Bernie, Eve & the Peacemaker/Montague Farm family; Paul & Nancy Gipe; Bob Fitrakis, Suzanne Patzer and our mystery webmaster at the Columbus Institute for Contemporary Journalism and www. Freepress. org, and all the good Free Press folks; Bobby Kennedy, Eddie Scher. and the Waterkeepers; Barry Zucker and Ohio Citizens Against the Mis-Use of Pesticides; Dennis Sandage; Chick Bornheim; Mark Hertsgaard; Avi Peterson; Lori Grace; Jim, Mary Beth & EON; Susie, Jonny & the Diamond Family; the Shamanskys; Schoffman-Stoff-Ehlers-Broder-Tirman-Martin-Butcher-Pane-Palmer-Clare-Whitbeck; Steve & Marilyn Strong; John Abrams; David Hughes; Bob Gough & Winona LaDuke; COUP, NREL, AWEA, ASES, ILSR, Green Power-Gen, GEO and the CWA; John Passacantando & the Greenpeace Rainbow Warriors; Mary Barley, Chris Ball, Paul & Sonja Jones and the Everglades Foundation; Jackie Jones, Alasdair Cameron and Renewable Energy World;.Dar Williams; Dennis & Elizabeth Kucinich; John Hall; Greg Palast; Leonard Shlain; Walt Musial; Norman Solomon; Bob Koehler; Paul Loeb; Carol Weis; Mitzi Bowman; Noel Abbott; Larry Fahn; Tom Manwell; Lionel DeLevingne; Lou & Judy Friedman; Art & Connie Hogarth; Pete & Toshi Seeger; Danny Goldberg, Ilene Proctor, Jason Salzman, Danny Schechter, June Golden, M.C. Miller, Guy Fisher; John Wilton; Wilbert the artist; and many more. To Kurt Vonnegut, Studs Terkel & Howard Zinn, for their endless inspiration. To Molly Ivins, our supreme Solartopian Goddess.

And, of course, with endless love to Susan & the Wasserwomen---Annie, Abbie, Julie, Shoshanna---and to our wonderful extended families, including Rachel, Yaakov, Yehudah & Aviva; Nancy, Phil, Journey, Joiwind, Amit, Lila-Bean & New Baby; Holly, Larry, Bobby & Jackie; Marilyn, Elliot & Haley; Mike & Giselle; Phyllis, Norman, George, Enid & Mel.

To Sig & Phyllis, now and forever.

And, above all, to *you* dear reader, for helping bring us to Solartopia!

Harvey Wasserman was thrilled to learn in 1973 that Northeast Utilities wanted to build a nuclear plant four miles from the communal organic Montague Farm (founded in 1968 as an offshoot of the legendary anti-war Liberation News Service).

Prompting the phrase "No Nukes," pioneer western Massachusetts Solartopians converted the proposed reactor site into a nature preserve.

After the first "Toward Tomorrow" renewable energy fair in Amherst in 1975, he served on the first media committee of the Clamshell Alliance, whose mass 1976-8 non-violent demonstrations helped cancel the proposed Seabrook Nuclear Unit Two. He helped organize the 1979 Musicians United for Safe Energy Concerts in Madison Square Garden, and spoke in 1994 for Greenpeace USA to 350,000 semi-conscious rock fans at Woodstock 2.

Harvey appears frequently on major media shows such as Lou Dobbs, Today, Phil Donahue, Thom Hartman, *All Things Considered, Democracy Now*, Peter B. Collins, and more. He is a radio talk host and columnist for www. freepress.org.

He and co-author Bob Fitrakis have been called by Rev. Jesse Jackson: "The Woodward and Bernstein of the 2004 election."

Harvey serves as senior advisor to Greenpeace and the Nuclear Information & Resource Service. He teaches history at two central Ohio colleges, and speaks regularly on campuses and to citizen groups throughout the U.S.

His Farmers Green Power Co. works on farmer/community-owned wind development.

He and his wife Susan have five daughters, two grandchildren and two grand-nieces.

Contact Harvey at: www.solartopia.org

Also by Harvey Wasserman

Harvey Wasserman's History of the United States
(www.harveywasserman.com) Introduced by Howard Zinn

A Glimpse of the Big Light: Losing Parents, Finding Spirit
(www.harveywasserman.com) Introduced by Marianne Williamson

The Last Energy War: The Battle Over Utility Deregulation
(www.sevenstories.com)

America Born & Reborn: The Spiral of U.S. History

Energy War: Reports from the Front

With Bob Fitrakis:
What Happened in Ohio?
A Documentary Record of Theft and Fraud in the 2004 Election
(www.thenewpress.com) also with Steve Rosenfeld

How the GOP Stole America's 2004 Election & Is Rigging 2008
(www.freepress.org and www.harveywasserman.com)

Did George W. Bush Steal America's 2004 Election?
(www.freepress.org) also with Steve Rosenfeld

Imprison George W. Bush and *George W. Bush vs. the Superpower of Peace*
(www.freepress.org)

With Dan Juhl:
Harvesting Wind Energy as a Cash Crop:
A Guide to Locally-Owned Wind Farming
(www.danmar.us)

With Dan Keller (Documentary Films):
Lovejoy's Nuclear War and *The Last Resort*
(www.gmpfilms.com)

With Norman Solomon, Bob Alvarez and Eleanor Walters:
Killing Our Own: The Disaster of America's Experience with Atomic Radiation
Introduced by Dr. Benjamin Spock

Also from www.harveywasserman.com

HARVEY WASSERMAN'S HISTORY OF THE UNITED STATES
Introduction by Howard Zinn

"A beautiful example of people's history…" from the introduction by Howard Zinn

"Harvey Wasserman is truly an original…" Studs Terkel

This much-loved cult classic from the Civil War to WWI is a mainstay for students and teachers in search of an alternative point of view---and a solid, exciting historic read.

"The Civil War made a few businessmen very rich" is the legendary opener on this wild ride from Robber Barons to radical Populist farmers, from Debsian socialist workers to Bohemian free lovers. Read it once… your view of US history will never be the same.

*By Harvey Wasserman * 216 pages * $18.00 * ISBN#09753402-0-4*

A GLIMPSE OF THE BIG LIGHT: LOSING PARENTS, FINDING SPIRIT
Introduction by Marianne Williamson

"A knockout"…Kurt Vonnegut

"A song for the soul"…Bonnie Raitt

"Beautiful, elegaic, swinging, a long medium-tempo ballad with passages of double time, like something Mingus might have played"…Ben Sidran

This passionate and powerful poetic excursion into grief and rebirth, loss and illumination is a soulful, symphonic recital of the passing of beloved parents and the spiritual journey that followed. It is a sweet, liberating rite of passage for all who seek.

*By Harvey Wasserman * 164 pages * $18.00 * ISBN#09753402-2-0*

HOW THE GOP STOLE AMERICA'S 2004 ELECTION & IS RIGGING 2008
By Bob Fitrakis and Harvey Wasserman

"Fitrakis and Wasserman are the Woodward and Bernstein of the 2004 Election …"
Rev. Jesse Jackson

The theft of Ohio 2004 was the crime of the century. Based in Columbus, Fitrakis and Wasserman warned eight months beforehand that the election was being rigged, then broke the story world-wide. This infuriating bullet-point compendium is the essential "on-the-ground" executive summary of how George W. Bush stole a second term.

*By Bob Fitrakis and Harvey Wasserman * 100 pages * $14.00 * ISBN#09753402-8-X*

www.harveywasserman.combox 09683 bexley, ohio 43209**fax (614)237-0420**

Printed in the United States
77932LV00002B/371-444